LAWRENCE IN DORSET

RODNEY LEGG

To Leslie

With Love & Best Wishes for 2,000

Ruth, Howell & Nain

DORSET PUBLISHING COMPANY   WINCANTON PRESS

NATIONAL SCHOOL, NORTH STREET, WINCANTON,
SOMERSET BA9 9AT

"After I'm dead they'll rattle my bones
about, in their curiosity." – T. E. Lawrence,
to Jock Chambers
[27 iv 29]

"He was one of those rare beings who
seemed to belong to the morning of
the world. His end would have pleased him –
a swift rush and a sudden passing." – Lord Lloyd,
at the funeral of
Lawrence of Arabia
[21 iv 35]

Publishing details. Second edition, revised and expanded, 1997. Published by Dorset Publishing Company at the Wincanton Press, National School, North Street, Wincanton, Somerset BA9 9AT.

Printing credits. Typeset by Julie Green. Printed by F. W. B. Printing, Bennetts Mead, Southgate Road, Wincanton, Somerset BA9 9EB.
Distibution. Trade sales distribution by Halsgrove, Lower Moor Way, Tiverton, Devon EX16 6SS. Telephone: 01-884-243-242.
International Standard Book Number. [ISBN] 0 948699 57 4.

Lawrence beside the rhododendrons at Clouds Hill on Brough Superior GW 2275, his last motorcycle: he was thrown from it in his fatal crash on 13 May 1935.

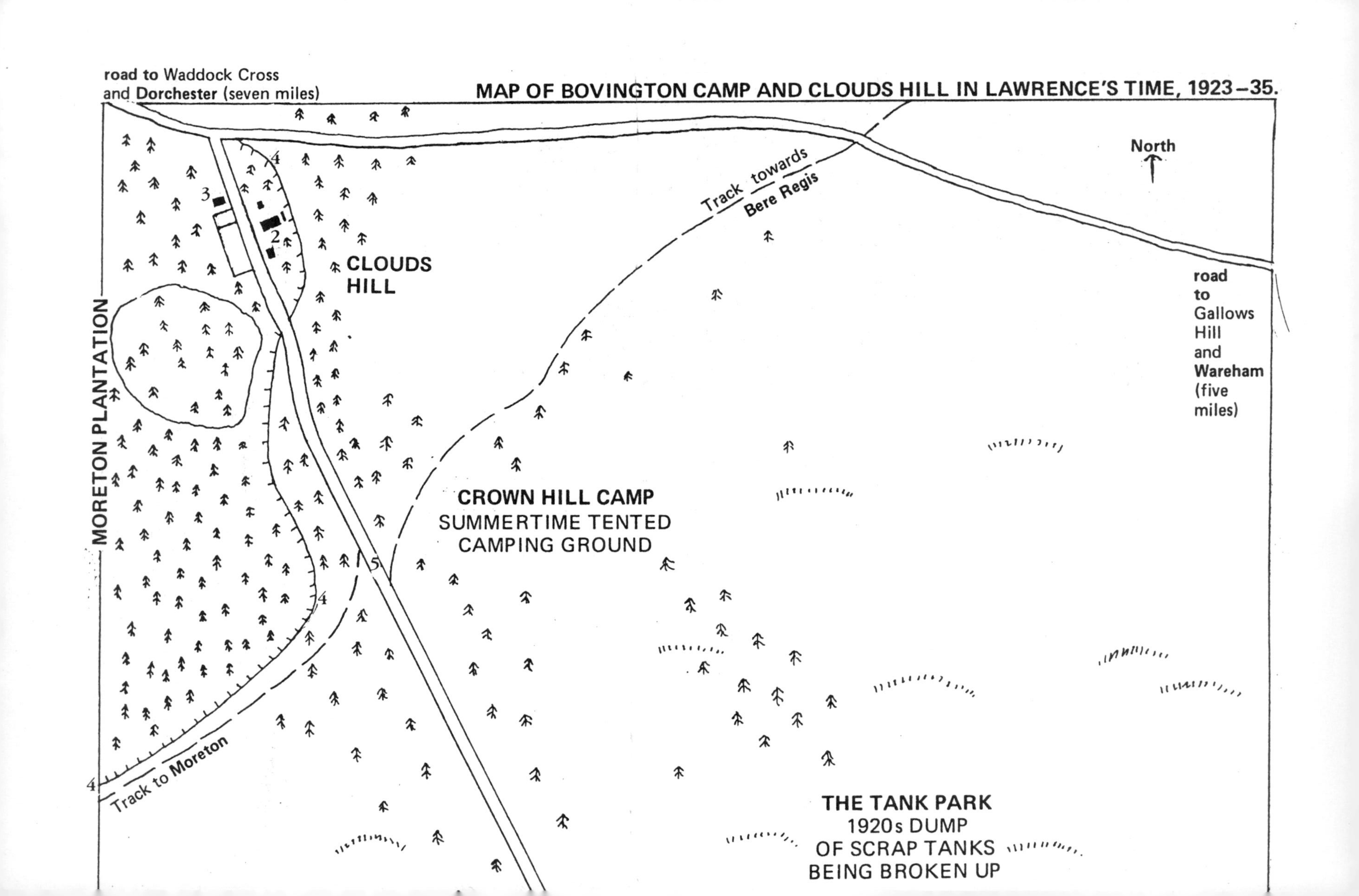
MAP OF BOVINGTON CAMP AND CLOUDS HILL IN LAWRENCE'S TIME, 1923–35.
road to Waddock Cross and Dorchester (seven miles)
North
Track towards Bere Regis
road to Gallows Hill and Wareham (five miles)
CLOUDS HILL
1
2
3
4
5
MORETON PLANTATION
CROWN HILL CAMP
SUMMERTIME TENTED CAMPING GROUND
Track to Moreton
THE TANK PARK
1920s DUMP OF SCRAP TANKS BEING BROKEN UP

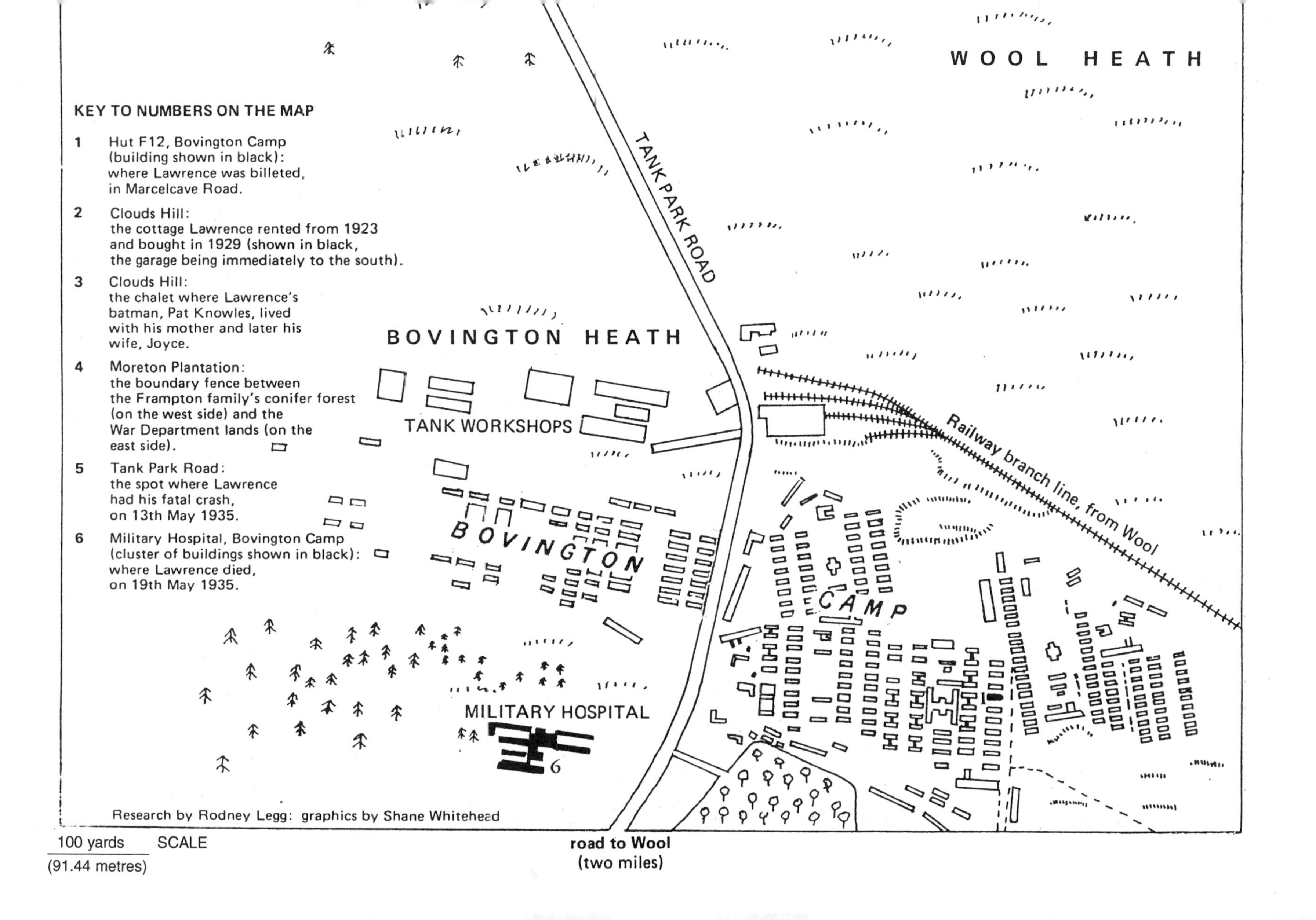

KEY TO NUMBERS ON THE MAP
1 Hut F12, Bovington Camp (building shown in black): where Lawrence was billeted, in Marcelcave Road.
2 Clouds Hill: the cottage Lawrence rented from 1923 and bought in 1929 (shown in black, the garage being immediately to the south).
3 Clouds Hill: the chalet where Lawrence's batman, Pat Knowles, lived with his mother and later his wife, Joyce.
4 Moreton Plantation: the boundary fence between the Frampton family's conifer forest (on the west side) and the War Department lands (on the east side).
5 Tank Park Road: the spot where Lawrence had his fatal crash, on 13th May 1935.
6 Military Hospital, Bovington Camp (cluster of buildings shown in black): where Lawrence died, on 19th May 1935.
WOOL HEATH
TANK PARK ROAD
BOVINGTON HEATH
TANK WORKSHOPS
Railway branch line, from Wool
BOVINGTON
CAMP
MILITARY HOSPITAL
1
6
Research by Rodney Legg: graphics by Shane Whitehead
100 yards SCALE
(91.44 metres)
road to Wool
(two miles)

Opposite
The classic Lawrence, posing as a Prince of Mecca, in a damaged photograph found and re-copied by the Daily Mail – though he came to tire of it, Lawrence willingly aided the creation of his own legend.

A gentle introduction

It was shortly before the centenary of the birth of Thomas Edward Lawrence that I came across the discarded notes for this manuscript by chance. I was searching for the one quotation about myself that I cherish, said by Jeremy Pope to my solicitor, Maurice Jensen, in the days when my Dorset County Magazine used its teeth: "This scurrilous rag-monger." This is from those days, in 1968, when I was fresh from four years' newspaper reporting and felt quite up to explaining the odd little Dorset mystery. Or rather gathering information for the book that my partner, Colin Graham, had decided to write about the crash which killed Lawrence of Arabia.

Colin never proceeded with its publication and during the two decades we were together it was a subject into which I ventured at my peril. I had my view, and he his. When Colin departed for an extended stay with his parents in Australia I was free to have my own opinions again. The material and its presentation is mine, though but for Colin I would never have stepped into the minefield that is T. E. Lawrence. Re-reading it I was surprised at the general lucidity though I have gone back to it with Ockham's razor to clarify crucial turns in the commentary. *Entia non sunt multiplicanda praeter necessitatem:* suppositions are not to be unnecessarily multiplied.

What unfolds moves the story from the public domain and into the secret history of the twentieth century. If in the process I largely ignore the sexual revelations of other biographers it is because I consider them a distraction. The man was great enough and interesting enough to sustain the damage. Even national heroes feel the need to do things in private; books of that kind diminish their writers rather than their subjects.

Here was the one man of the modern age who restored romance and drama to the tarnished image of war. In peacetime Dorset his cottage retreat could not contain his hyperactive mind. That the times were changing, and Europe was to be conditioned for a return to what had been its natural state – id est, warfare – was a cause for excitement rather than apprehension. Things tend to happen, however, in a society which is dusting its chess-pieces for battle. Even an unsuitable king may find himself edged into abdication with an American divorcee, Mrs Simpson, providing the convenient moral excuse for a disposal that was caused by political indiscretion. I see Lawrence too as a problem piece from the same box; an unpredictable knight.

It is to politics rather than emotions that I turn for my answer to the puzzle.

Oxford, 1910: T. E. Lawrence with his brothers. Left to right – Thomas Edward Lawrence (known as 'Ned', born 16 August 1888); Frank Helier Lawrence ('Frank', born 7 February 1893, killed leading an advance on the Western Front in 1915); Arnold Walter Lawrence ('Arnie', born 2 May 1900; would survive T.E.); Montagu Robert Lawrence ('Bob', born in December 1885, would survive T.E.); William George Lawrence ('Will', born 10 December 1889, killed in the Royal Flying Corps, being shot down after less than a week in France, 1915).

The story so far

Thomas Edward Lawrence was born in 1888 at Tremadoc, Caernarvonshire. The actual day is recorded as 16 August 1888 but when someone claimed significance in the date of their birth, Lawrence would respond: "Ah, but I was born on Napoleon's birthday!' That, however, was the previous day; Napoleon Bonaparte was born on 15 August 1769. T. E. Lawrence was the product of a liaison between an Anglo-Irish aristocrat and the family governess. That T.E. and his four brothers were illegitimate is relevant to the story that follows in that it was an offence against Victorian society and a stigma he felt in life. T.E. was known as "Lawrence II' (being the second eldest) at school and "Ned" at home. After moving around Britain, Jersey and France the family settled at 2 Polstead Road, Oxford, when T.E. was eight. The brick and tile house has its blue plaque:

This house
was the home
of
T. E. LAWRENCE
(LAWRENCE OF ARABIA)
from
1896–1921

Behind a cupboard door in a downstairs sitting room the present owner, Mrs Elinor Phillips, preserves the pencil marks the boys made to chart their growth. "Ned" at 21 was at the bottom, left behind by his brothers. When he was twelve he had broken his leg in a fight at school and only belatedly allowed it to receive medical attention. It was suggested that this may have stunted his growth. Anyway, he reached only 5 feet $5^1/_2$ inches, though to anyone meeting him he seemed even shorter.

What he lacked in stature he compensated for in mental agility and guts. He was brilliant, and he tuned his mind into a computer of a retrieval system that could outclass just about everyone he met. It won him a scholarship to Jesus College, Oxford, in 1907 and by 1909 he had progressed from cross-Channel bicycling holidays to a major study of the crusader castles of Syria that won him a first class honours degree in 1910.

He was back in Syria in 1911 helping to dig up Carchemish, a Hittite lost city on the Euphrates, for the British Museum, during which time he perfected photography, surveying, and a working knowledge of Arabic. Field Marshal Kitchener commissioned a survey of the Sinai Desert in 1913 and Lawrence and his Carchemish supervisor, Leonard Woolley, were chosen so that the mapmaking could be carried out under the pretext of archaeology to avoid alerting the Turks.

Hereon he would be one of the most exciting and enigmatic lives of the century. On the outbreak of war in 1914 he was an intelligence officer in Cairo, where his slovenly dress and behaviour – a studied indifference and indolence – was offset by brilliant reports on the Arab nationalists. These disparate factions he galvanised into the Arab Revolt against the Ottoman Empire. Captain T. E. Lawrence slipped with boyish delight into Arab dress and on to a camel's saddle as he led his fierce Bedouin tribesmen, the nomads of the sands, against the might of the Turkish army. He adopted guerilla tactics, blowing up their railway lines and trains, and developed a panache for hit and run raids after which his camel brigade disappeared into the desert. The mosquitoes became phantoms.

When the press caught up with the Hejax Expeditionary Force they found the most colourful and romantic figure of the Great War and a story that went round the world in newspapers and moving pictures to restore something of the thrill of decent warfare to nations weary of the carnage in the trenches. Lawrence's rise was meteoric, to use an appropriate metaphor because meteors are seen as they fall to earth. From Captain he became Major and was then made Lieutenant-Colonel. He was attached to General Francis Wingate's staff and then to General Edmund Allenby's victorious Egyptian Expeditionary Force which took Jerusalem on 9 December 1917.

The classic action of the Arab Revolt was its capture on 6 July 1917 of the strategic town of Akaba, at the northern end of the Gulf of Akaba, which is the arm of the Red Sea which juts into the Holy Land. Here the Turks were expecting an attack from the sea. Instead the Arabs rushed their outposts to

The man and his moment; a tulip bomb blasts the Turks' Hejaz railway. It was the stuff of romantic legend and the media would oblige. Here in the campaign that Lawrence himself dismissed as "a sideshow of a sideshow" the Arab Revolt brought glamour back into warfare. It was all a long way from the carnage of the Western Front – which claimed two of Lawrence's brothers.

the north, from the direction of Maan, and proceeded to sweep into Akaba.

Their decisive final contributions to the campaign began on 8 August 1918 when the Arab Army turned inland and took Medawera on the Hejaz railway, 65 miles south of Maan, with the capture of 120 Turks, two field guns, and three machine guns. On 16 September 1918 the Arabs destroyed a bridge and tore up the railway line 15 miles south of Deraa. The Arab Army now numbered 8,000 and were the serious worry for the Turks on their eastern flank.

The Arab Revolt then caused the final defeat of the Turks – by taking

their attention away from the coast. Instead the Turks looked towards the desert and expected the main attack to be spearheaded by Lawrence's Arabs who were around Kasr el Azrak. The anticipated thrust was a move towards Damascus via Deraa. Another hero convinced the Turks: Richard Meinertzhagen dropped a brief-case whilst pretending to be shot. It contained a fabricated document about an attack from the east. This stratagem was a brilliant success and enabled Allenby to prepare an offensive above the Mediterranean with three mounted divisions, and 383 guns. The presence of a force on that scale was unknown to the Turkish

1 October 1918: Lawrence in the front of the Rolls as his Arab Army captures Damascus – the Turkish sideshow was being brought to a close. Opposite, in 1921: the diplomatic sequel. Damascus is handed back to the French but its Hashamite leader, Faisal I, is moved sideways by the British and given the throne of Iraq. Conference picture with Colonial Secretary Winston Churchill (front, third from left) and Lawrence (top right).

headquarters. It was therefore with complete surprise that the coastal forces attacked at dawn on 19 September 1918 and broke through both lines of Turkish trenches.

After the break-through on the coast the Arab Army continued its in-roads from the desert. On 24 September the Arabs were 14 miles south-east of Deraa; they took the town on 27 September. Nothing now could keep them from their prize – the city of Damascus.

There on 1 October 1918 Lawrence and his irregulars – chanting his name as they rendered it, "Aurens! Aurens!" – entered the Syrian capital ahead of the regular army. Here the glory started to fade for Lawrence as he realised that international politics would override the moment because Syria was a French sphere of interest where the British would betray their pledges to the Arabs and restore the pre-war status quo.

Colonel Lawrence returned to Britain to a London Gazette listing of the Distinguished Service Order and Companionship of the Order of the Bath. These he went along to Buckingham Palace for the purpose of rejecting – embarrassing George V and offending officials by telling the King he could not accept any honours whilst His Majesty's Government reneged on the promises it had given the Arabs in exchange for their services in battle. From the French he did accept the Croix-de-Guerre; only to pin it to the collar of a dog that was allowed to roam through the streets of Oxford.

Faisal I, Lawrence's leading Arab friend, who took command of the Arab Revolt at Medina, had been proclaimed King of Syria in March 1920 by the Syrian National Congress but was deposed by General Henri Gouraud,

France's one-armed High Commissioner in Syria. Lawrence was able to engineer a British compromise which in 1921 placed Faisal on the throne of Mesopotamia, which was now known as Iraq. This country was under British mandate as a trust territory on behalf of the League of Nations until 1932 it became an independent state. This much achieved, in 1922, Lawrence walked out from the Arab affairs desk of the Middle East division of the Colonial Office.

He had rejected his fame to the face of his King in one of the most calculated insults the Palace has suffered. Lawrence's other indignities were to himself. He turned down prestigious and highly paid offers and deliberately sought alternatives that would negate his talents. A monastery did not seem inappropriate but the Royal Air Force would do as a practical alternative. What the doctors saw failed to impress; he was too small, underdeveloped, and had scars allegedly caused by recent flagellation.

Even then Lawrence did not give up. Having got an Arab a crown or two, he was determined to talk his way into the R.A.F. where Air Chief Marshal Sir Hugh Trenchard, an old associate, was conveniently the Chief of Air Staff. The second time around the doctors had no say in the matter, and Lawrence calling himself John Hume Ross, became Aircraftman 352087 Ross at the R.A.F.'s Uxbridge Depôt on 30 August 1922.

Four months later Ross was back in civvy street. The wolf-pack of Fleet Street had sniffed out the story of the unusual recruit and put Uxbridge under siege. The situation was insufferable because Hillingdon House at Uxbridge had the headquarters staff of the Air Defence of the United

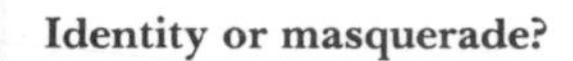

Identity or masquerade?

Left **Captain Thomas Edward Lawrence of the British Army in the Great War: head-dress of the Palestine theatre.**

Opposite **Will the real T. E. Lawrence stand up? Posing for Flight-Lieutenant Stanley Smetham as Aircraftman T. E. Shaw of the Royal Air Force, at Miranshah, India, in 1928.**

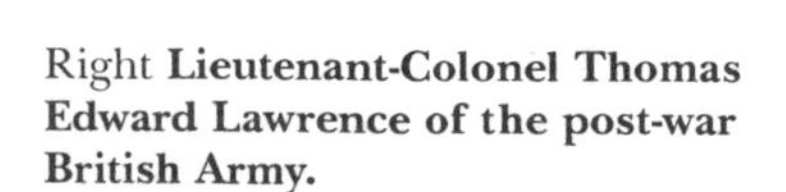

Right **Lieutenant-Colonel Thomas Edward Lawrence of the post-war British Army.**

Kingdom.

Their loss was Dorset's gain. The Ross name was abandoned and the next was Shaw, out of admiration for the playwright and author George Bernard Shaw, with his real forenames, Thomas Edward, being restored. The 1923 enlistment was as Trooper Shaw of the Tank Corps which had its headquarters base on the Dorset heaths midway between Dorchester and Poole. The Colonel who had taken the desert by storm would graduate as a quartermaster's storeman.

He 'did not know what fear was'

In 1968 I corresponded with but one of the Dorset men who had fought with Lawrence in the desert campaign; that war was then going through its fiftieth anniversaries, and its survivors would soon be extinct.

Lieutenant-Colonel Archibald Donald Strange-Boston, who had been born at Bucknowle in the Isle of Purbeck and served in Palestine in the Great War, wrote to me from Shreveport, Louisiana, on 9 April 1968: "Lawrence was a wee mon, I'd say about 5 feet or 5 feet 1 inch. Always had dirty feet in sandals. Dressed like an Arab merchant. Wore the princely form of headgear. Generally concentrated his looks on his feet – but when he did look up, and at you, you wished he had not for it was like a sharp knife going through butter.

"I believe Tom was one of the very few men I have ever known who did not know what fear was. All that rot about him was made up except for what happened at Deraa (held by the Turks) and what happened there he could not prevent. What single man (even a heavy-weight) could hold off twenty men? He came back silent – ill spiritually detached and in shock.

"I do well remember him saying to me: 'There are two things I am afraid of – an untruth, and an injustice.'

"There was a barber in Wareham named R. W. Strange (no relation of ours) who used to cut his hair. I spoke to Strange when I was over there in 1932, and he cut my hair. 'Did I ever know Colonel Lawrence?'

"I replied 'Slightly'. Then Strange went into a barber-shop gossip about Lawrence. I was tired and did not listen, but Strange knew him rather well."

Lawrence and Faisal

Pre-war contacts between T. E. Lawrence and Faisal [1885-1933], the third son of Husein ibn-Ali, were reported by Phillip Knightley in the Sunday Times of 26 April 1981. The evidence came from the French Army archives and contradicted the account in the *Seven Pillars of Wisdom* where Lawrence describes their meeting in 1916, after Husein – the Grand Sherif – had fired the first shot in the Arab Revolt, out of the window of his home in Mecca, at the nearby Turkish barracks.

Lawrence writes that having eliminated the Grand Sherif and his other sons as suitable leaders of the Arab rebels, he rode up country to Faisal, in Medina, "and found in him the leader with the necessary fire". He stood as a tense, white figure, framed in a black doorway: "I felt at first glance that this was the man I had come to Arabia to seek – the leader who would bring the Arab Revolt to full glory..."

Knightley proceeded to call this "an elaborate fiction", outlining the French intelligence reports, in the Chateau de Vincennes archives, near Paris, which had been discovered by Dr Robin Bidwell of Cambridge University. These were from two French officers, Lieutenant Doynel de St Quentin who was attached to the British forces in Egypt, and Adjutant Lamotte who had a similar role monitoring Faisal's column in the desert. Lamotte stated that Faisal and Lawrence not only knew each other before the war but had worked as fellow conspirators in a secret nationalist committee in Damascus.

Lawrence was there in 1909 and 1911, with the latter being the more likely date for such an involvement, as he was with his mentor David Hogarth; the keeper of the Ashmolean Museum at Oxford and a British agent.

Such a link could explain Lawrence's resolve to ensure that Faisal was the first to arrive at the liberation of Damascus, on 1 October 1918. Indeed he would for a short time be its ruler, being proclaimed King of Syria by a national congress in March 1920 but deposed by the French, under General Gouraud, in July that year.

Instead the British gave him Mesopotamia and called it Iraq, under an interim mandate from 1921 until independence was granted in 1932.

Faisal never forgave either European power for how they rewarded him and his Bedouin for having helped them kick the Turks out of the desert. He was ousted from his own nation by the French and treated as a vassal by the British.

Knightley quoted a British diplomat who dealt with Faisal after the war: "He was very bitter about what he considered was the way in which he had been treated by both British and French and made some wounding remarks about British character in general."

We might know more about all this from three French folders catalogued as "Notes du Capitaine Lawrence" but Bidwell found they were missing from their box. So too was a fourth file on Lawrence's relations with Faisal. That had been "Passed to P."

'Seven Pillars': in memory of an Arab boy

Lawrence's life enshrined a single love – his devotion for an attractive brown-eyed Arab donkey-boy he had met at Carchemish in 1911 and brought back to London and Oxford for the summer of 1913. From him Lawrence was able to perfect his Arabic and for the lad the cultural exchange was a

camera. They also swapped clothes and laughingly photographed the result in one of the peaks of the great emotional high of Lawrence's existence. In the Desert Revolt, Lawrence would risk the lad – Salim Ahmed, otherwise known as Dahoum – in espionage around Turkish positions. It was to typhoid, however, that he would lose him in 1918.

His first detailed letters about the boy are as revealing as anything that he

S.A. interchanged with T.E.L.:

Dahoum, whose proper name was Salim Ahmed,
is seen opposite at Carchemish in Lawrence's clothes –
note that Middle Eastern archaeology came complete with revolver.
This clothes swapping was the only time the camera captured
an exuberantly happy moment in Lawrence's life.
They were smiling at each other – Lawrence took Dahoum's picture,
and he photographed Lawrence.

would openly commit to paper.

In July 1911 Lawrence wrote to Mrs Rieder at the American Mission School in Jebail about Dahoum, which means "The Dark One", saying he was going to ask Miss Fareedah el Akle of the school for some books for the lad: "It is a great thing to be an employer of labour. I have had quite a success with our donkey-boy, who really is getting a glimmering of what a brain-storm is. He is beginning to use his reason as well as his instinct: he taught himself to read a little, so I had very exceptional material to work on but I made him read & write more than he ever did.

"You know you cannot do much with a piece of stick & a scrap of dusty ground as materials. I am going to ask Miss Fareedah for a few simple books, amusing, for him to begin on. Remember he is to be left a Moslem. If you meet a man worth anything you might be good enough to remember this? A boy of 15 ... I would be vastly obliged."

Lawrence wrote home from Carchemish on 12 September 1912: "Dahoum is very useful now, though a savage: however we are here in the feudal system, which gives the overlord great claims: so that I have no trouble with him: he wrestles beautifully, better than all of his age and size."

For all his contrary clues, or rather his willingness to let others have their false assumptions, Lawrence hints at the boy's identity in a letter from Bovington Camp to Robin Buxton on 22 September 1923:

"S.A. was a person, now dead, regard for whom lay beneath my labour for the Arabic peoples. I don't propose to go further into detail thereupon."

In the same letter he explains the source of the title of his book:

"The *Seven Pillars of Wisdom* is a quotation from *Proverbs:* it is used as title out of sentiment: for I wrote a youthful indiscretion-book, so called, in 1913 and burned it (as immature) in '14 when I enlisted. It recounted adventures in seven type-cities of the East (Cairo, Bagdad, Damascus etc.) & arranged their characters into a descending cadence: a moral symphony. It was a queer book, upon whose difficulties I look back with a not ungrateful wryness: and in memory of it I so named the new book, which will probably be the only one I ever write, & which sums up & exhausts me to the date of 1919."

Though he took care to hide the significance of Salim Ahmed from his potential biographers, Robert Graves in particular, Lawrence was unguarded in a letter to Aircraftman R. M. Guy: "People are not friends until they have said all they can say, and are able to sit together at work, or rest for long without speaking. We never quite got to that but we were nearing it daily – and since S.A. died I haven't experienced any risk of that happening."

Phillip Knightley and Colin Simpson, whilst preparing their *Secret Lives of Lawrence of Arabia*, which grew out of a series of Sunday Times features in 1969, found references to an Arab who died of typhoid in September 1918 "before we reached Damascus", and who Lawrence saw dead "to be held one moment ... before earth's soft hands would explore your face". Tom Beaumont, an armoured car machine-gunner, recalled Lawrence saying "I loved that boy".

"When he turned back," Beaumont continued, "I could see that he had been weeping. I overhead the bodyguards talking and I caught the Arabic word for death and I saw them make gestures like Lawrence holding Salim in his arms."

On his aeroplane flight across Europe Lawrence would pencil the most unhappy lines of his life at the back of his copy of Sir Robert Vansittart's *The Singing Caravan*, a note which Knightley and Simpson would discover in the Lawrence papers in the Bodleian Library at Oxford:

"I wrought for him freedom to lighten his sad eyes: but he had died waiting for me. So I threw my gift away and now not anywhere will I find rest and peace.

"Written between Paris and Lyons in Handley Page."

It is, as the Sunday Times reporters point out, an obvious first attempt at a dedication; I cannot share Desmond Stewart's alternative assumption that these were thoughts on the recent death of his father. It has the essence of agony contained within those beautiful words at the start of *Seven Pillars*:

To S.A.

I loved you, so I drew these tides of men into my hands
and wrote my will across the sky in stars
To earn you Freedom, the seven-pillared worthy house,
that your eyes might be shining for me
When we came.

Death seemed my servant on the road, till we were near
and saw you waiting:
When you smiled, and in sorrowful envy he outran me
and took you apart:
Into his quietness.

Love, the way-weary, groped to your body, our brief wage
ours for the moment
Before earth's soft hand explored your shape, and the blind
worms grew fat upon
Your substance.

Men prayed me that I set our work, the inviolate house,
as a memory of you.
But for fit monument I shattered it, unfinished: and now
The little things creep out to patch themselves hovels
in the marred shadow
Of your gift.

The hurt remained, at the intensity of sadness reflected by the original note written in the aeroplane, and Lawrence would never find an adequate substitute. The loss of Salim Ahmed was the continuing tragedy in his life. From that point Lawrence's life was a mess. The inner turmoil would spill into his letters and admissions, and caused the creative imperative for a literary record of the Desert Revolt. It would be an epic in the style of Homer and Virgil though with touches of Charles Montagu Doughty's *Travels in Arabia Deserta* [1888]. Only in that form could the history live up to Lawrence's expectations. Driving himself to fulfill that destiny Lawrence needed to regard it as an endurance necessary to preserve the memory of his youthful and loyal admirer. He dedicated the *Seven Pillars of Wisdom* to "S.A." with the most perfect opening words that have been inspired for any dedication in the English language: "I loved you, so I drew these tides of men into my hands and wrote my will across the sky in stars ..."

Lawrence realised he was creating an "S.A." enigma in the league of the "W.H." of Shakespeare's sonnets and encouraged the confusion by writing that the dedication was to "an imaginary person of neutral sex". That was indeed his view of Dahoum; to Lawrence he was a creation largely of the imagination which he now inhabited – the one perfect human being who could be beyond sex. Having "S.A." as the riddle of his sands would, Lawrence realised, constantly draw attention to the existence and importance of Salim Ahmed, his Dahoum, and was quite the reverse of an attempt at concealing his identity.

Where was Lawrence on 21 November 1917 ?

The importance of Dahoum is second only to the events of 21 November 1917, which was the night of the traumatic sexual experience of Lawrence's life, when by his own account he was captured whilst on an espionage mission behind enemy lines at Deraa, the junction town on the pilgrims' railway between Medina and Damascus. He was brought before Hajim, the Turkish Bey, who had him stripped and propositioned him. Lawrence wrote that he resisted; was bitten at the neck; had a bayonet worked around the flesh over his ribs; was stretched along a bench and flogged with a Circassian riding whip. He experienced a "delicious warmth, probably sexual" and was then subjected to further humiliations by three soldiers, one of whom "rode me like a horse".

The loss of his "bodily integrity", he wrote to Charlotte Shaw in 1924, would make him "forswear decent living and the exercise of my not-contemptible wits and talents".

It is not new to question the Deraa incident, even to suggest it was a fantasy of Lawrence's invention, but Lawrence James took the matter a stage further in 1990 with *The Golden Warrior*.

He attempts to prove that on the night of 21 November 1917, Lawrence was at Akaba. Earlier that day he had travelled from there in a car of the 10th Motor Section of the Royal Field Artillery, landed only hours before from Egypt, on a reconnaissance of Wadi Yutm. He was accompanied by Colonel Joyce. The War Diary of the R.F.A. Motor Section, document WO 95/4415, records: "22.11.17. Carried out reconnaissance with Col P. Joyce and Col Lawrence up Wadi Yetm (sic)."

James acknowledges that the diary was not written up until April 1918 but says that key dates such as embarkation (Marsa Matruh, 11 November) and disembarkation (Akaba, 21 November) are most unlikely to be wrong. Neither, he argues, would the event of the first excursion into the desert, particularly as it was for the benefit of two colonels, of whom Lawrence was already a living legend.

The following morning, Lieutenant Samuel Brodie of the 10th Motor Section first met Lawrence at Joyce's tent, according to the memories in *T.E. Lawrence by His Friends*. This is undated, but refers to the day after disembarkation.

Even if the drive to Wadi Yutm was that day, 22 November 1917, it would still preclude Lawrence being in Deraa the night before.

James believes that the Deraa incident was fabricated and offers this reason for its invention: "He was making a coded statement about his own sexuality; something like this had occurred to him, but at another time and in different circumstances."

'Mind-suicide' of enlistment

David Garnett saw in Lawrence's bizarre decision to enlist in the ranks a mental masochism to match the studied indifference to physical pain which he had shown for a broken leg as a schoolboy in 1904 and would display again by neglecting a smashed arm in 1926: "There are rational and logical explanations why Lawrence enlisted, but the final and most compelling was an irrational urge to submit and to subject himself to men most obviously his inferiors."

"Mind-suicide" would be Lawrence's own phrase for it; not that the War Office readily accepted this unusual request, from its most famous officer hero, to return to the ranks and start again. Lawrence stressed to his friends the refuge he needed in the anonymity of the army. He had just tried and failed to do the same thing with the Royal Air Force, though in the high-brass surroundings of its headquarters Depôt on the edge of London, and this time his friends succeeded in talking the War Office into transferring the experiment to a lower-profile hutted camp that specialised in tank maintenance and training. These vehicles were introduced to Dorset, the British Army and to war only seven years earlier, and they were confined to a piece of desolate heath-land a hundred and twenty miles from the capital.

Clearance came from the War Office via the Adjutant General: "I have received this morning a letter from Elles who is prepared to consider your proposal ... He asks you to write to him at HQ Tank Training Centre, Bovington Camp, marked personal ..."

Tank Corps and Clouds Hill

Lawrence enlisted into the Tank Corps on 12 March 1923 at 7875698 Private Thomas Edward Shaw and joined its 1st (Depôt) Battalion at Bovington Camp, on the Dorset heaths between Wool and Bere Regis [Ordnance Survey map reference SY 830 890]. On 18 October 1912, by the King's warrant, the Corps became the Royal Tank Corps. By then Lawrence thought it anything but royal: "The Army is muck, stink, & a desolate abomination."

A mile north of the camp, on a knoll smothered in rhododendron scrub – an alien weed of the heath, introduced from the Himalayas and managing textbook stuff in the ecology of invasions – he found in September 1923 a tiny two-up, one-and-a-half down former gamekeeper's cottage which dated back to the start of the nineteenth century. This spot, on the edge of the Victorian pinewoods of the Moreton Plantation [at map reference SY 823 909], lay in the empty wastes of the parish of Turners Puddle and carried the magic name Clouds Hill. It is about 225 feet above sea level.

Not that the surroundings were quite all they might sound. The road from Clouds Hill then had a sharp kink just below the cottage before dropping into the straight section that went all the way, as it still does, to the Tintown huts that were Bovington Camp. From here however, in 1923, the view was marred in the near-distance by rows of rusting tanks in their hundreds. These obsolete machines had been brought home from the Western Front and a team of breakers would spend the entire decade working their way through them. The handful that survived this and later exhortations for scrap are now displayed in the Great War hangar of Bovington Tank Museum. The Tank Park, as it was known, is now a pinewood in the valley two hundred yards east of the Clouds Hill road, which was called Tank Park Road, [Ordnance Survey map reference SY 829 903] half a mile south-east from Lawrence of Arabia's cottage.

This he rented from the Frampton family, the owners of the Moreton Estate to which all this part of Dorset, including previously the military lands, belonged. The rent was two shillings and sixpence a week; half-a-crown. Lawrence sold the most valuable of his war treasures, his princely gold-hafted Arabian dagger, to his friend Lionel Curtis, and used the money to repair the cottage roof and floors.

It was a fair exchange. From the start Lawrence enthused about Clouds

Clouds Hill: its cottage, with 'Dorsetshire to look at' as Lawrence put it.

Hill and compared its natural beauty with the self-inflicted indignities and obscenities of army life as he found it at Bovington Camp. This was the Egdon Heath of Thomas Hardy's novel *The Return of the Native* which in 1927 would inspire Gustav Holst's tone-poem *Egdon Heath*.

An anecdote from Lawrence to Lionel Curtis summed up the degrading life he found in the Tank Corps. It was written on 19 March 1923, in what seems to be the earliest surviving letter from Lawrence at Bovington Camp.

"They're the sort who instinctively fling stones at cats," he remarked to one fellow.

"Why, what do you throw?" the soldier asked.

Corporal Alec Dixon gives the best vignette of Lawrence at Bovington: "I never saw him to relax. He was surely a man with 'ants in his pants', if ever there was one. When walking about the Camp his normal bearing was very noticeable for, except when on a drill parade, he did not swing his arms as he walked in the approved manner – an oddity which singled him out from all of us. He walked 'all of a piece' as it were, with an air of tidiness; his arms were close to his body and his toes well turned out, though not exaggeratedly so. As he walked he appeared to see no one about him; his head was slightly tilted and the blue-grey eyes steady, looking neither to the right nor left."

Clouds Hill was his "earthly paradise" where eventually he hoped for a "lifetime of Sundays" – not that I wholly believe him because Sundays are not for racing minds – and he found "the perfect beauty of this place becomes tremendous by its contrast with the life we lead, and the squalid huts we live in, the noisy bullying authority of all our daily unloveliness.

"The nearly intolerable meanness of man" – here he means the view of Bovington Camp from Clouds Hill – "is set in a circle of quiet heath, and budding trees, with the firm level bar of the Purbeck Hills behind." Ignoring, as I have said, the graveyard of tanks spilling across the heath in the near distance, but poets have that licence.

"The cottage is alone in a dip in the moor, very quiet, very lonely, very bare. A mile from camp. Furnished with a bed, a bicycle, three chairs, one hundred books, a gramophone of parts, a table, many windows, oak-trees, an ilex, firs, rhododendron, laurels, heather. Dorsetshire to look at."

The unlovely side of life with which Lawrence humiliated himself, as a Colonel in the British Army pretending to be an ordinary raw recruit, was centred on Hut F-12 of Tintown as everyone locally then knew Bovington Camp. Lawrence's hut was in Marcelcave Road, which has since ceased to exist. It lay beside what is now the east wall of the north-east wing of the Sandhurst Barrack Block [Ordnance Survey map reference SY 834 892], built in 1938 at 165 feet above sea level to provide quarters for 650 men.

Of the hut he wrote, "there is an animal reek here which keeps me awake at night with horror that mankind should be like it". Lawrence also complained of the frightening lack of driving abilities in the trainees who threw their armoured cars around the heath and left him with a shivering nervousness that turned at nights to fever and delirium in which he "talked like rivers" in his sleep. Letter-writing seems to have been the masturbation of Lawrence's mind; he wrote at his best from turmoil and frustration and the imprisonment in F-12 was crucial to the final efforts that were necessary to push the manuscript of the *Seven Pillars of Wisdom* into print. Picasso understood the feeling. He was once asked to sign a petition demanding the release of imprisoned Russian authors. "Why?" he asked. "They write better in prison."

Clouds Hill was allowed only partially to mitigate the suffering. It was a spartan existence inside four walls that had music to comfort the mind and warmth to relax the body: "In my cottage is no food, and no bed. At nightfall there is a flea bag, and I lie on the preferred patch of floor in either room. The ground room is for books, and the stair room is for music: music being the trade name for a gramophone and records. There are five acres of rhododendrons and fires every evening from their sticks."

From the start of life in the Tank Corps, Lawrence was still thinking words, as he made clear on 16 April 1923 to his publisher, Jonathan Cape:

"Thanks for the word about translating. I'd like to make however-few pounds, and it would be nice to play with words again. Squad-drill is a little

Bovington Camp: Lawrence's view of it in words and contemporary pictures, which are from Lieutenant-Colonel George Forty's 'Bovington Tanks'. Tintown, the place was then called.

The road stretching out of the camp is that going northwards, across the heath to where Lawrence's Clouds Hill cottage was the next building – a mile away in physical measure and a million miles in terms of its lifestyle.

Clouds Hill: the tiny gamekeeper's home a mile north of Bovington Camp in the Dorset heathland parish of Turners Puddle which is now preserved by the National Trust and appears on the Ordnance Survey map as 'Lawrence of Arabia's Cottage'. It stands in a small grassy clearing amid oaks and an impenetrable tangle of rhododendron scrub. Lawrence's 'Does not care' inscription is above the door. The pictures are by Colin Graham, taken for his major photographic study of 'National Trust Dorset'.

heavy on the mind." To Edward Garnett on 12 April 1923 he was writing about George Bernard Shaw reading the manuscript of the *Seven Pillars of Wisdom* and continues:

"Yes I'm at Wool – camped not by Lulworth, but on Bovington Heath – Hardy's Egdon. We go to Lulworth for gunnery later on, after the end of drills.

"I've seen Hardy twice, but have no other adventures barring one race up to London (2 hrs. 55 mins.) to see [Augustus] John's show. I got back, perforce, in 2 hrs. 45 mins (126 miles each way), and was in place to answer my name for both noon and evening roll-calls. A good ride, or race, rather. Everyone thought it impossible for me to get up and down in the afternoon.

"The camp authorities are very narrow towards us recruits – giving no leave till August, and few spare afternoons. Lulworth not allowed without a pass – but I risk it and run down occasionally for a smile at the sea. Too cold to bathe – except in the rain.

"My number is 7875698: Name Pte. T. E. Shaw. Address is Mr T. E. Shaw, c/o H. Smith (Stationer), Bovington Camp, Wool, Dorset.

"I've really struck bed-rock – or basc material – this time. The army is unspeakable: more solidly animal than I believed Englishmen could be. I hate them, and the life here: and am sure that it's good medicine for me.

"Revise the book? Do you know, I've now reached the happy point of being really sorry that I ever wrote it! Apologies: I must be exasperating to work with: but what can I do about it? Any idea of working over it again must wait. Projects of epochal writings flit – or flash, through my head. If I can take one on the wing I'll look at it carefully ... but this atmosphere is hostile to everything."

Lawrence had already set in motion a request, via the young poet, ex-Captain Robert Graves [1895–1986], to meet "old Hardy" who was the literary eminence not only of Dorset, but of England. He wrote from Sir Herbert Baker's flat at the top of 14 Barton Street, Westminster, on 20 March 1923:

"So I'm now a recruit in the Tank Corps. Conditions rough too. However there is a certainty and a contentment in bed-rock. I wanted to ask you ... we are near Dorchester and I run about on wheels (when they take their eyes off us) ... do you think old Hardy would let me look at him? He's a proper poet and a fair novelist, in my judgement, and it would give me another milestone passed if I might meet him. Yet to blow in on him in khaki would not be an introduction. You know the old thing, don't you? What are my hopes? youuuuuuuurs T.E."

Graves received a positive response from Max Gate, Hardy's self-designed Victorian villa beside the Wareham road out of Dorchester, and Lawrence wrote immediately to Florence Hardy, on 25 March 1925:

"Dear Mrs Hardy, A letter from Robert Graves (to whom I had written) tells me I'm to get into communication with you. It feels rather barefaced, because I haven't any qualifications to justify my seeing Mr Hardy: only I'd very much like to. *The Dynasts* & the other poems are so wholly good to my taste. It adds to my hesitation that I'm a private in the Tank Corps, at Wool, and would have to come across in uniform. You may have feelings against soldiers, also I'm therefore not master of my own time.

"They let us off on Wednesdays, Saturdays and Sundays at noon: and I have a motor-cycle so that getting over to Dorchester is only a matter of minutes. I must be in camp again at 9.30 p.m.: but between that & noon on any of those three days for the next three months I should be free, if you are good enough to offer me a time. The deepest apologies. I'm suggesting that you take a great deal of quite unwarrantable trouble.

"Yours sincerely T. E. LAWRENCE. (In case you like R.G. enough to reply, please address me 7875698 Pte. T.E.Shaw, Hut F.12, B Company, 1st Depôt Battalion, Tank Corps, Bovington Camp, Wool. I dropped the 'Lawrence' part of me six months ago. TEL.)."

In fact they met on a Thursday, 29 March 1923, as Lawrence records in a letter the following day from "Tank-town" to Eric Kennington [1888–1960], the illustrator of *Seven Pillars of Wisdom:*

"You're a hero – a ...ero they'd say in this place: which is Hardy's Egdon Heath. The Heath is good ... and I saw Hardy yesterday: paid for seeing him too, for it meant cutting a parade! However it was worth it, and I'm going again, if ever he asks me. His weakness in character-drawing is a reflection of himself. A very sensitive little man: faded now: with hope yet that mankind will give up warfare. He felt incredibly old to me."

On Easter Saturday, 31 March 1923, the army was sensible enough to cut fatigues short by an hour or two and leave Lawrence free at 10 a.m. "So," he wrote to David Hogarth the following day, "I leaped for my bike & raced her madly up the London road: Wimborne, Ringwood, Romsey, Winchester, Basingstoke, Bagshot, Staines, Hounslow by 1.20 p.m. (three hours less five minutes). Good for 125 miles: return journey took 10 minutes less!

"In London I went straight to the Alpine Gallery. [Augustus] John's thing of you is wonderful. Might have been drawn by a drunken giant, after eating a mammoth. I doubt whether he's ever done anything quite so strong before ...

"Yours isn't beautiful: it's savage: but the performance of it is so masterly that one forgives the rudeness & splash of the chalk-work. Was he drunk? Anyway for once John has worked with his brakes off, letting everything rip. It is (as it should be) the biggest thing in my portrait gallery. What shall happen to it? John sends it to Barton St. when the show ends. It remains mine till reproduced, of course; I don't know if you'd like it in your house. One's Self-portraits are rather hard to live up to, I fancy. Besides Mrs Hogarth won't like it.

"I hope you'll see the show. The other things are mixed, but the average is surpassing. The big composition is almost mad. I felt my eyes dancing with it, & preferred to look at Mme. Suggia, who is just a great portrait. It's good that John should boast such a middle age.

"The wall with you in the middle is all spotted with drawings of me in various incarnations. One looks like a budding sergeant ... It's a pity Trenchard didn't see it before he decided to sack me.

"Don't like the Army. It's so unlike the R.A.F. No feeling for it in the ranks. Everyone is here because he is broke, & they want nothing & hope nothing from their service, except food, pay, and little work. In the R.A.F. people talked of their technical jobs, & of flying, & of the future of the air, half their time.

"No leave from here till August, & uncertain then. So won't reappear yet, unless I buy out, which on one head I'd be glad to do. I should have said that I bust the bike, just outside camp. Ran over a broken glass bottle at speed, burst front tyre, ran up a bank & turned over. Damage to self nil; to bike somewhat. There goes my power of breaking bounds!'

The first outsider to experience the Lawrence magic at Max Gate was the poet and novelist Walter de la Mare [1873–1956]. He had the Lawrence seal of approval. From the start Mrs Hardy would forewarn Lawrence on whom he was likely to meet, and he wrote to her on 21 May confirming his appearance at tea-time on Saturday 26 May 1923:

"De la Mare is known to me only by his books – but he should be delightful, if he lives up to them: and most good people are better than their books.

"It sounds greedy, always to come when you ask me; but your house is so wonderfully unlike this noisy room that it is difficult to resist, even for its own sake; and then there is Mr Hardy, though you mustn't tell him so, for the thrill is too one-sided. He has seen so much of human-kind that he must be very tired of them: whereas for me he's Hardy, & I'd go a long way to see the place where he had lived, let alone him living in it. There, you will think me absurd: but still I'll arrive on Saturday!'

De la Mare recalled the experience on a BBC wireless programme in 1955 and said that he too was in a way prepared for the encounter, though he seems to have remembered the day as a Sunday. Hardy teased him all afternoon: "The very next afternoon – a Sunday – he told me rather diffidently after lunch, but with Florence Hardy's nod of concurrence, that a prince was coming to tea. I did not turn a hair, I hope; nor ask which prince. I merely ran through, as far as I could, the complete Victorian Royal Family and decided against each one of them in turn.

"Then I remained on tenterhooks. Round about four there came a ring at the bell. And as if a Jinnee had trumpeted in my ear, I realised instantly that on the doorstep was Colonel Lawrence. And Colonel Lawrence was, of course, a Prince of Mecca."

There were, however, some aspiring literati who were not going to have the privilege and pleasure of meeting the Desert Prince.

On 3 June 1923 Lawrence made his excuses for avoiding a Max Gate

Sunday, in a note dropped off when he was en route for Plymouth. The reason was that Max Beerbohm, remembered as a caricaturist [1872–1956] would be there. He had made it clear in a letter to Edward Garnett on 26 August 1922 that he found the man contemptibly light-weight: "If I'd aimed low I could have hit my target as squarely as Max Beerbohm or Belloc hits it: but their works are only a horrid example, and I'm much happier to have gone high [with *Seven Pillars*] then flopped than not to have tried, or to have tried half-measures."

Lawrence used as his excuse a hut-mate at Bovington Camp, Private Butler:

"Such a feast to miss! There is a little homesick man, called Butler, in the hut with me; and I promised a week ago to take him home to Plymouth to tea with his people, on our first fine Sunday. He has been looking at the weather every morning since, and I can't disappoint him – because he wouldn't known who Max Beerbohm and the G.B.S's [Bernard and Charlotte Shaw] were. I'm most sorry. This will be pushed in as we pass; our torrent of noise returning will rush past your windows tonight about 9 p.m. Hard luck I call it."

Probably both reasons were equally valid. Private Butler, one assumes, must have had his charms and been good worldly company for a day-out that took precedence over Max Gate. Obviously he was going to prefer as a treat a visit home to his parents rather than a silent afternoon at Dorchester listening to people who might as well have been from another planet.

Lawrence was however at Max Gate on Sunday 29 July 1923; greeted by Wessex the dog and finding the house also hosting Siegfried Sassoon [1886–1967] and Edmund Blunden. Blunden, a poet and literary critic [1896–1974], is credited with these jottings in *The Great Victorians* but I have also found them in print, attributed, in 1935, to Sylvia Norman:

"Wessie barks in the drive.

"S. Sassoon, T. E. Lawrence in private soldier's uniform, E. Blunden.

"Mrs Hardy enters, doesn't shake hands.

"Tea, small talk.

"Lawrence, marked politeness.

"T. Hardy enters, 'brushes' hands, re-seats the assembly.

"Lawrence is seated on the sofa – 'for once'.

"T.H.: 'No sofas at the camp?'

"Lawrence asks questions about Toller Down [former fairground on the top of the downs between Maiden Newton and Crewkerne].

"T.H.: 'Often bicycled there."

"Lawrence discloses to Sassoon the whereabouts of his tribesmen.

"Mrs H.: 'My husband wants to hear you speak some Arabic.'

"L.: 'Can only speak kitchen Arabic.'

"L. translating a book on the life of a Californian pine-tree [surely the bristlecone, some of which are 2,000 years old] from the French, in order to pay for his motor-cycle.

"T.H.: 'Why don't you translate something from the East?'

"Lawrence: 'I have the strongest feeling that there is nothing in the East...'

"I think this must have been the occasion when L. and T.H. discussed the *Iliad* ...

"Lawrence, talking to us, expressed a poor opinion of T.H.'s novels, except the descriptive parts; did not recognise the 'homegrown quality' in T.H.'s poems; was astonished at the spectacle of Hardy as a poet in his old age."

On 8 September 1923 Lawrence thanked Robert Graves for the introduction to Thomas Hardy:

"For the ticket which gained me access to T.H. I'm grateful to you – probably will be grateful always. Max Gate is a place apart: I feel it all the more poignantly for the contrast of life in this squalid camp."

In return Lawrence told Graves much about the nation's premier living novelist and poet, despite his reservations that "T.H. is an experience that a man must keep to himself".

Hardy was "so pale, so quiet, so refined into an essence, and camp is such a hurly-burly. When I come back I feel as if I'd woken up from a sleep: not an exciting sleep, but a restful one. There is an unbelievable dignity and ripeness about Hardy: he is waiting so tranquilly for death, without a desire or ambition left in his spirit, as far as I can feel it: and yet he entertains so many illusions, and hopes for the world, things which I, in my disillusioned middle-age, feel to be illusory. They used to call this man a pessimist. While really he is full of fancy expectations."

Hardy was so self-assured that he could have Homer and Sir Walter Scott as his mental companions:

"Yet any little man finds this detachment of Hardy's a vast compliment and comfort. He takes me as soberly as he would take John Milton (how sober that name is), considers me as carefully, is as interested in me: for to him every person starts from scratch in the life-race, and Hardy has no preferences: and I think no dislikes, except for the people who betray his confidence and publish him to the world.

"Perhaps that's partly the secret of that strange house hidden behind its thicket of trees. It's because there are no strangers there. Anyone who does pierce through is accepted by Hardy and Mrs Hardy as one whom they have known always and from whom nothing need be hid."

Other aspects of this revealing letter will be mentioned later as the Lawrence–Hardy(s) relationship unfolds.

Lawrence was noticed riding out of Dorchester by W. G. L. Parsons, a telegram messenger in the town: "On more than one occasion I have seen him leaving Max Gate on that magnificent twin cylinder 'Brough Superior' motor-cycle, often admired the machine whenever it was observed in the streets of Dorchester, and marvelled that a man of such short stature as Lawrence could handle the heavy machine in such a way as he did. The size of the machine seemed to add emphasis to the rider's short stature."

By 15 August 1923 it was to and with Hardy's wife, Florence, that Lawrence was experiencing a meeting of minds. She had found the manuscript of *Seven Pillars of Wisdom* uplifting but this was an aspect Lawrence at least pretended to shy away from:

"Your remark about 'uplift' has been puzzling me. One of my reasons for suppressing the book was that I believed it to be perverse and disturbing; a book likely to harm rather than [do] good to the normal person who would read it. It is meant to be the true history of a political movement whose essence was a fraud – in the sense that its leaders did not believe the arguments with which they moved its rank and file: and also the true history of a campaign, to show how unlovely the back of a commander's mind must be.

"So what you said cuts right across my belief, & has puzzled me. Will you tell me what you would do – publish or leave private – if yourself or Mr Hardy had written such a book? Apologies for bothering you: but the value of the book would give me an income which would keep me out of the army: and I'm wondering since Sunday whether perhaps I may be able to enjoy it.

"Another matter. *If* Mr Hardy does such things, would he inscribe me copies of his thin-paper *Poems & Dynasts*. I have them and could bring them across. I know it's a vulgar desire; but I live in vulgar company: and they would be very precious possessions."

Inside the Cottage

Clouds Hill is the Lawrence shrine. It is preserved much as it was, with the addition of the inevitable picture displays, though these are tastefully contemporary in the form of snapshots behind glass panels rather than the brasher kind of modern educational aids. It maintains the atmosphere of the withdrawn, secluded retreat that Lawrence wrapped around himself in the 'Twenties. Everywhere around it are the rhododendrons behind which the Private Shaw could hide. Five acres of them were presented to the nation, to the National Trust, by Arnold Walter Lawrence in 1938 as a memorial to the brother who had been twelve years his elder.

Opposite, down the slope from the road was the rural chalet that was home to Pat and Joyce Knowles who became caretakers for the Trust. It was absorbed into the Trust's holding in 1957, and replaced by a virtual mansion in 1996. The land in the Trust's care is now seven and a half acres, on the south side of the junction of the road from Bovington Camp with that from Waddock Cross to Gallows Hill.

Clouds Hill cottage, of painted brickwork with a tile roof, has two upper rooms and one-and-a-half rooms down as I have written – or rather, it is more squeezed than that with the upstairs being a loft with a skylight and a window in the gable end. The place is pint-sized, though the tendency of photographers to use wide-angle lenses gives misleading impressions of roominess. It was built for the gamekeeper of the Moreton Plantation and makes its debut on the Frampton estate records in 1808.

Lawrence's physical stamp on the building is the inscription he inserted above its door. "Nothing matters," has been the general view of what it says, in Greek. When the press asked Lawrence for its translation he replied "Not your concern" or "Don't bother me". It is in fact "Does not care" which, Lawrence told E. M. Forster, he had taken from the story of Hippocleides who had become the successful but drunken suitor of Princess Agarista. He danced on the table then stood on his head. "You have danced away your wife," Agarista's father told him. "I don't care," Hippocleides replied. The story comes from the Greek historian Herodotus.

The door had a wrought-iron knocker in Lawrence's time; surprisingly as it is almost an invitation to inquire within.

Inside are three main rooms with the one downstairs being a book room. It now has Lawrence's sleeping bag, marked "Meum" – he did not like fussing about with sheets – rather than being set out like a conventional

ΟΥ ΦΡΟΝΤΙΣ

'Does not care' – Lawrence took the words from the Greek historian Herodotus and put them above his door. The picture below is another of Colin Graham's shots of the main room downstairs – from the fireplace towards the window, with 'Meum' (Lawrence's sleeping bag) in the centre.

living room. Its furniture is Lawrence designed, with a leather-covered divan, leather-covered cushion, and matching armchair. The cushions are reversible. Lawrence also sketched out the design for the stainless steel bookrest, whilst he was working with launches at Hythe on Southampton Water. Likewise the wrought-iron three-piece fender with the stainless steel top is to his concept.

The bookcases and the photographs are a posthumous re-creation of the key titles and moments of Lawrence's life, though through thirty-six of his own negatives taken during the Arab Revolt, from October 1916, and eight that date back to the gathering of his material for the 1909–10 thesis that would be published in 1936 as *Crusader Castles* by the Golden Cockerell Press. There are also photographs of the intermediate period in the desert, the archaeology at Carchemish and Lawrence's room there.

The other photographs are of the later Lawrence, taken during the period covered by the present book though in places like Hythe (June 1934) and Hornsea, Yorkshire (February 1935) rather than at the cottage.

The pictures, and indeed the bookcases and their selection of titles by, about, or read by Lawrence, were assembled by Flight-Lieutenant R. G. Sims. There are nine of the actual illustrations prepared by Eric Kennington for the first privately-printed edition, limited to a few invited subscribers, of *Seven Pillars of Wisdom* that went to press in 1926. These include the line drawings "A Literary Method", "Kindergarten", and "Wind". There are also

Clouds Hill: a main room downstairs, with fireplace.
Photograph showing the room as it is now preserved, taken by Colin Graham.

the Kennington pastels of Emir Abdullah, Ali ibn el Hussein, and Auda abu Tayi, and three of his imaginative pictures for the book: "Thinking"; "Strata"; "Dysentery".

Other pictures are of Lawrence, by Augustus John who did his quasi-official portrait for the Tate Gallery. There are photographs of the bronze head Eric Kennington sculpted for St Paul's Cathedral. A Kennington chalk drawing was dubbed by Lawrence "The Cheshire Cat".

The four framed brass rubbings were made by Lawrence at Elsing, in Norfolk, between 1906 and 1909, at the start of his creative life, and came to the house from his mother in 1954. There is a framed sketch of a 37ft. armoured target launch, in the design of which Lawrence participated on Southampton Water.

On the mantelshelf are a pair of three-beamed candlesticks made by Lawrence's colleagues on the launch project, and presented to him when he left the Royal Air Force for the final time in 1935. Lawrence's bust, in the corner to the left of the fireplace, was made by Eric Kennington in 1926, and presented to the cottage by R. V. Buxton. Lawrence liked it. "Magnificent," he told Kennington, "there is no other word for it. It represents not me, but my top moments, those few seconds in which I succeed in thinking myself right out of things." The upstairs, attic room is known as the music room – being dominated by Lawrence's E.M.G. gramophone with its huge horn. It was effectively the sitting room. There is an oak folding-leaf table and two

Clouds Hill: the main room upstairs, as it is preserved by the National Trust – overleaf is the view the other way, seen from the fireplace.

Clouds Hill: two other shots of the main room upstairs, dominated by its E.M.G. horn gramophone, also photographed by Colin Graham for his book on 'National Trust Dorset'.

chairs. The coffin stool is from Max Gate, having been given to Lawrence by Florence Hardy after the author's death; a touch of morbidity both Thomas and T.E. would have appreciated.

The other seat is a leather settee, with cushions. The fire has a wrought-iron fender and beside it is a box for the rhododendron sticks that were used as firewood.

The painting of the heath at Turners Puddle, northwards from Clouds Hill, is by Gilbert Spencer. On the stairway descending to the downstairs room is Kennington's pastel of Lawrence.

The other upstairs room of the cottage is variously known as the bunk room or the eating room. It does have a ship's bunk with spring mattress though Lawrence's second sleeping bag, "Tuum" for visitors, disappeared in the 1960s with one of the self-invited latter-day sort who came after the cinemas released David Lean's blockbusting epic, the 1962 Panavision film, *Lawrence of Arabia*. The room has a small mahogany table and a mirror. On the table are three glass domes which mark the site of Lawrence's bread, butter and cheese.

In this room is a framed embroidery of the emblem of 204 Squadron R.A.F., based on the photograph of a cormorant which Lawrence took on Southampton Water. He also chose the motto, "Praedam mari quaero". An Arab robe hanging in the room was bought from an Arab by Sydney Cockerell, who gave it to Lawrence for use as a dressing-gown. Lawrence gave it to George Bernard Shaw, who also used it as a dressing-gown. It eventually came back to Cockerell, who then gave it to Sir Alec Guinness.

The sparse dietary situation at Clouds Hill was outlined to A. E. Chambers on 3 August 1924: "No food, except what a grocer at the camp shop and canteens provide. Milk. Wood fuel for picking up. I don't sleep here, but come out at 4.30 p.m. until 9 p.m. nearly every evening, and dream, or write or read by the fire, or play Beethoven or Mozart to myself on the box. Sometimes one or two of the Tank Corps slaves arrive and listen with me ... but few care for such abstract things."

E. M. Forster recalled the cottage in an article in The Listener on 1 September 1938: "In those days the two bottom rooms [the smaller one later became the bathroom] were full of firewood and lumber. We lived upstairs, and the sitting room there looks now much as it did then, though the gramophone and the books have gone, and the fender with its bent ironwork has been remodelled. It was, and it is, a brownish room – wooden beams and ceiling, leather-covered settee. Here we talked, played Beethoven's symphonies, ate and drank. We drank water only or tea – no alcohol ever entered Clouds Hill ... and we ate – this sounds less romantic – out of tins. T.E. always laid in a stock of tinned dainties for his guests ... T.E. slept in camp, coming out when he could during the day as did the rest of the troops."

Corporal Alec Dixon, from Bovington, described a typical Clouds Hill gathering:

"T.E. was an expert at 'mixed grills' where men were concerned. He presided over the company, settling arguments, patiently answering all manner of questions, feeding the gramophone, making tea, stoking the fire, and by some magic of his own, managing to keep everyone in good humour.

"There were many picnic meals (stuffed olives, salted almonds, and Heinz baked beans were regular features) washed down with T.E.'s own blend of China tea. Some of us used chairs, others the floor, while T.E. always ate standing up by the end of the wide oak mantelshelf which had been fitted at a [low] height convenient for him."

Life at Clouds Hill was basic, or at least for literary visitors. Yet F. J. Stratton, who ran the butcher's shop opposite the Post Office at Bovington Camp, happens to mention in passing in the course of his recollections of the day of Lawrence's death, a taste that is a little out of keeping with pseudo-vegetarianism: "He came to the shop as he had done many times when home here, to buy two chops for his lunch."

Consistency for Lawrence was a matter of the utmost inconsequentiality. It was to be his lasting joke at the expense of historians and his annual biographers who are accustomed to taking such things seriously. I know someone with the same endearing trait who also displays the Lawrence chuckle, that half-suppressed giggle one sometimes finds in boys who never grow up.

Mr and Mrs White ran the fish and chip shop at Bovington Camp. They told Wareham historian Harry Broughton that Lawrence was partial to fish and chips and finnan haddock. The latter would be bought for him by Mrs Knowles, the mother of his neighbour, Pat Knowles. If Lawrence came in and there was anyone else in the shop he would leave rather than queue. Mrs White overcame the problem by ignoring the other customers and instantly making up a parcel of fish and chips as if he had ordered them in advance.

Lecture notes in Arabic

Privates Arthur Russell and "Posh" Palmer were Lawrence's usual companions at the cottage. The lasting memory for the officers of their unusual recruit was that he took lecture notes in Arabic, or Greek as they thought it to be. The content was more likely to be something that stirred in Lawrence as he glanced at the tank-scarred sands around Bovington and returned in his mind to Arabia.

The massive manuscript of *Seven Pillars of Wisdom* had been posted to George Bernard Shaw for his comments in September 1922; it was still with him, without much constructive feedback having resulted, when Lawrence moved into the Clouds Hill cottage in September 1923.

Opposite **Bovington Camp: Lawrence of the Tank Corps reading a newspaper, probably outside hut F12 in 1923-24, with one of his new comrades looking on.**

Bovington life: condemned by Lawrence in his own hand, in a letter to Sydney Cockerell.

the army is dyeing me khaki by degrees, & I don't know that I'm any longer much company for real people. At least I feel that way, so shall abstain till I'm different.

At Bovington: 'No longer company for real people'

Lawrence wrote to Sydney Cockerell from Bovington Camp, on 22 October 1923 that "the army is dyeing me khaki by degrees, & I don't know that I'm any longer much company for real people. At least I feel that way, so shall abstain till I'm different."

The alleged affair with a Lance-corporal

Avoiding "real people" was one thing but somewhere in the sub-strata of Bovington life there may have been opportunities for some relief.

The barrister Robert Cecil Romer Maugham, second Viscount Maugham, records in his autobiography a sexual advance he fended off after a sergeant-instructor who had been at Bovington Camp in the 1920s produced a bottle of rum in a room above a public house in 1939. Maugham was then twenty-three and the soldier was trying to seduce him via an erotic story he told concerning T. E .Lawrence. This Maugham disbelieved, but it had details which would coincide with later highly-publicised revelations:

"When Colonel T. E. Lawrence was at Bovington under the pseudonym of Shaw, he had made friends with the instructor – who was then a lance-corporal. One evening he had invited the lance-corporal to drink with him. He had then persuaded the lance-corporal to whip him and then to penetrate him.

"As he gave the unpleasant details of the evening he had spent with Lawrence, the sergeant-instructor became visibly excited. Soon he was stroking my thigh. It was difficult to get out of the room without offending him."

This was the Private Lawrence that Lawrence Durrell and others sensed and detested – as with Durrell's 1935 comment, "what a disgusting little thing he was. His own personality decreased as the saga grew. What a little neuter, ripping and goring his body because he loathed it so ... a sort of nasty child."

Private Arthur Russell had seen the wheals on Lawrence's beaten back and was shown the bayonet scar on his stomach as they went into the sea to swim at Arish Mell, near East Lulworth. Lawrence told him the mutilations dated from his rape by the Turks at Deraa.

'Top-speed through these unfit roads'

The one carnal pleasure Lawrence did admit to enjoying was the fast-moving air across his mind and body as he challenged Dorset's sub-standard road system with the world's top-class motor-cycles.

Statistically, the risk factor of the high-speed life Lawrence lived on the Dorset lanes must have been somewhere equal to the odds of surviving the desert war against the Turks. In both cases adrenalin flowed, as Lawrence confirmed in a letter to Lionel Curtis in 1923: "When my mood gets too hot and I find myself wandering beyond control I pull out my motor-bike and hurl it at top-speed through these unfit roads for hour after hour. My nerves are jaded and gone dead, so that nothing less than hours of voluntary danger will prick them into life: and the 'life' they reach then is melancholy joy at risking something worth exactly 2 shillings 9 pence a day."

Describing a visit to Wells Cathedral in June 1923, where he had ridden one Sunday after church parade in Bovington, Lawrence writes of a white-frocked girl playing on the grass at the foot of the tower: "I knew of course that she was animal: I began in my hatred of animals to balance her against the cathedral: and knew then that I'd destroy the building to save her.

"That's as irrational as what happened on our coming here, when I swerved at 60 m.p.h. on to the grass at the roadside, trying to save a bird which dashed out its life against my side car. And yet had the world been mine I'd have left out animal life upon it."

His skill and daring on the motor-cycle were widely admired at Bovington Camp. Corporal Alec Dixon writes in his *Tinned Soldier* that "70 miles an hour was nothing to Shaw, and couldn't that little bloke ride a motor-bike"? It was "Broughie" Shaw that he became nicknamed after taking Dixon and other men out on the powerful machine that had been improvised by its maker George Brough to meet his requirements.

On 27 June 1923 Lawrence wrote to his mentor David Hogarth that life in the Royal Tank Corps was not that awful: "It is probably not worse than the reality of any other unit. It's only that the R.A.F. is much better."

He would become increasingly determined to secure a transfer back to the Air Force.

'The utter loneliness of his life'

Ernest Altounyan, an Armenian, was the friend who understood Lawrence as well as anyone. Lawrence had disappeared but a boy told Altounyan that he was down at the river, and following this information he intercepted Lawrence on Wareham bridge. It was to be a moment of truth.

"As he approached I saw again that hunted look which I had last caught in Dover Street. He was afraid for a moment that I was going to ask him where he had been. It was as though he mistrusted the felicity of the evening and could not quite believe my respect and understanding of his need for absolute freedom. I never realised so keenly as I did at that moment the utter loneliness of his life.

"It was as though he had fallen into the habit (he who was so disdainful of all habits) of never expecting complete intimacy, however great the host of his devoted friends. 'I have never loved anyone,' he wrote to me once, 'or hardly ever: lands and peoples – yes'; meaning that he had never experienced an affection which he felt to be undamaging to his or the other's freedom.

"I said nothing, but after breakfast, getting up every particle of courage, I attacked, accusing him of cowardice in personal relationship. 'Don't retreat from me,' I sad at last in despair. He looked at me dully and then asked me to come and see his motor bicycle. We never doubted each other again; but I saw now what he meant when he had said the night before: 'I haven't had much kick out of life; those days in Carchemish were the best.' By the merest accident of my own make-up I had stumbled on the truth. No one has ever lived so much alone."

Corporal Alec Dixon, who was serving with the Tank Corps when Lawrence arrived at Bovington Camp, recalled his moodiness for John E. Mack's *A Prince of Our Disorder* on 25 June 1967: "Solemnity and an air of melancholy distinguished his behaviour during his early months at Bovington Camp." In his book *Tinned Soldier*, Dixon compared Lawrence's methodical discharge of his duties, "efficiently and quietly, in a manner that contrasted oddly with the clamorous and slapdash methods of his younger companions".

Turned down Christmas with Thomas Hardy

The abstinence from people continued through Christmas Day in 1923 when Lawrence stayed at Clouds Hill. He had been invited by the Hardys to spend the day at Max Gate, their Dorchester home, but, he wrote to Sydney Cockerell, he had declined: "It is not good to be too happy often."

Lawrence explained to Cockerell that he did "rations and coalyard" duty so that the others would be "free for their orgy ... Xmas means something to them. My pernickety mind discovers an incompatibility between their joint professions of Soldiers and Christians." Another letter, to R. M. Guy, notes: "Xmas – spent alone in my new-old cottage – has been a quiet time of simply thinking."

What the Hardys had was a more elaborate excuse in a letter to Mrs Hardy that Lawrence had written on 22 December 1923: "I waited to see if I could: and I'm afraid I can't. It's a good thing because it would feel intrusive to go to lunch on Christmas day. However I would probably have fallen to it, only that I'm without transport. The ancient & splendid bicycle was borrowed (without leave) by a villager who rode her ignorantly, & left her, ruined, in a ditch. It saved me the pang of selling the poor beast, but also it shuts me unhealthily close to camp: – and so I'm trying to persuade the maker of it to supply me another! I'll hope to see you and Mr Hardy soon."

Lawrence allowed himself to be persuaded to go to Max Gate for lunch on 30 December. George Bernard Shaw and his wife, Charlotte, were there as well. Lawrence stayed for the afternoon.

Clouds Hill
Moreton
Dorset.

19.3.24

Dear Cockerell

Miss Mew: too much emotion for her art, for her intellect, for her will. Such intensity of feeling is a sign of weakness. She is a real poet .... but a little one, for the incoherency, the violence of over-wrought nerves

Lawrence the misogynist: demolishing sad poetess Charlotte Mew.

Eric Kennington's cartoon of Lawrence as a character assassin: his literary method.

"Tell me about Max Gate," Robert Graves would ask him.

"I can't," Lawrence replied, but he did, as I have already shown. Max Gate was at times as much part of the Dorsetshire escape as Clouds Hill itself: "It is strange to pass from the noise and thoughtlessness of sergeants' company into a peace so secure that in it not even Mrs Hardy's tea-cups rattle on the tray: and from a barrack of hollow senseless bustle to the cheerful calm of T.H. thinking aloud about life to two or three of us."

Thomas Hardy was then 83 and Lawrence was a young man of 35. It seemed to him that the novelist was still living in the Dorset of Napoleonic times. That, to Hardy, had been the real Great War.

"Then he is so far-away. Napoleon is a real man to him and the country of Dorsetshire echoes that name everywhere in Hardy's ears. He lives in his period, and thinks of it as the great war: whereas to me that nightmare through the fringe of which I passed has dwarfed all memories of other wars, so that they seem trivial, half-amusing incidents."

By the end of 1923 Lawrence was already figetting for a transfer out of the Royal Tank Corps and had suggested to Sir Hugh Trenchard [1873–1956] that he might go absent without leave, to which the Air Chief Marshal had replied, "you must not be a defaulter or you will get kicked out. Do not be an ass! If you start being a defaulter it will be impossible for me to help you or for you to help yourself."

Trying to get back into the Royal Air Force would become a continuing obsession for Lawrence over the next couple of years.

'I'm frigid towards women'

As for Lawrence's notorious dismissal of the feminine half of the human race there is sufficient evidence from an exchange of letters with Sydney Cockerell. Lawrence was typically misogynous when he wrote from Clouds Hill on 13 January 1924 that he had not yet come across the work of a particular contemporary poet: "Haven't heard of Charlotte Mew: but all the women who ever wrote original stuff could have been strangled at birth, & the history of English literature (& my bookshelves) would be unchanged ..."

He was, however persuaded to give her a chance but when he wrote back to Cockerell, again from Clouds Hill, on 19 March 1924, he found his prejudices confirmed. He adds, gratuitously, a rider that he is anyway frigid towards women, after observing that Mew [1869–1928, by suicidal ingestion of disinfectant] shows "too much emotion for her art, for her intellect, for her will. Such intensity of feeling is a sign of weakness. She is a real poet ... but a little one, for the incoherency, the violence of over-wrought nerves does much to harm her powers of expression ... only the passion is molten: the form, the thought, the music, these are unresolved, to be guessed at, or worse, to be supplied by the reader if his passion is set burning with sympathy with hers. I'm frigid towards woman, so that I can withstand her: so that I want to withstand her."

Lawrence the misogynist could go much further. "Being a mechanic," he told Robert Graves, "cuts one off from all real communication with women." As for the thought of anyone enjoying the painting of them, he was puzzled. He asked the artist Eric Kennington: "Do you really like naked women? They express so little." He wouldn't even trouble himself to show polite token interest in the pile of drawings of nudes that were the obligatory peep-show in Augustus John's studio.

Kennington found it difficult coping with Lawrence when he lapsed into one of his nihilistic moods: "Everything was attacked. Life itself. Marriage, parenthood, work, morality, and especially Hope. Of course, we suffered and were unable to cope with the situation."

Lawrence was on his way to making devoted friends and vehement detractors. Some accepted him, as did John Buchan [1875–1940], the adventure writer and wartime Director of Information for Lloyd George, who earn a knighthood and be created first Baron Tweedsmuir: "I am not a very tractable person, much of a hero-worshipper, but I could have followed Lawrence over the edge of the world. I loved him for himself, and also because there seemed to be reborn in him all the lost friends of my youth."

Those words shine through the Lawrence legend as freshly now as when Buchan wrote them in *Memory, Hold-the-Door*. Equally well written, but devastating as a denouncement, were those honed by Malcolm Muggeridge for the New York Times of 10 May 1964 in which he just about calls T. E. Lawrence the personification of the Devil: "What could be more extraordinary than the survival of this cult, which flourishes more as his lies and attitudinising are made manifest? He is superlatively a case of everything being true except the facts. Who more fitting to be a Hero of Our Time than this, our English Gent, our Sodomite Saint, with Lowell Thomas for his Satyr and Alec Guinness to say Amen?"

Lawrence was openly homosocial in that he relished male companionship. Of those male friends who were homosexual the most eminent who came to Clouds Hill was Edward Morgan Forster [1879–1970]. Not that he was one of Lawrence's young admired – Forster was nine years his senior. Like Lawrence his was to be an enduring fame, with such titles as *Where Angels Fear to Tread*, *A Room with a View*, *Howard's End*, *The Celestial Omnibus*, *The Eternal Moment* and *A Passage to India*.

'Of the few entirely satisfactory people in the world'

On 28 March 1924 Lawrence warned Florence Hardy that in two days, on Sunday 30 March, he would introduce Private "Posh" Palmer to life at Max Gate:

"I was promising myself the delight of coming over next Sunday, wet or fine: and now, thanks to your letter I'll presume to bring Palmer with me. He likes all the novels: *Jude* & *Tess* particularly. Mr Hardy won't approve. *The Dynasts* did not come his way until recently (through me): and he hasn't yet ended them. Till then I won't question him upon his taste: but he's a prose-reader first.

"I didn't like mentioning him at Max Gate, because it seems an unworthy thing for us to besiege it in our numbers: me first: Russell second: Palmer third. That isn't the purpose for which your hedge of trees grows thick. However it is too great a pleasure for us to refuse. Forster was very good: came up twice, & talked perfectly. I hope his new book [*Aspects of the Novel*] will be what he deserved."

It seems Lawrence went alone after all because Palmer had a cold and Hardy had to be kept away from as many germs as possible. Anyway,

Lawrence left Dorchester with a parcel addressed to "Colonel Lawrence" as Mrs Hardy always insisted on calling him; indeed Thomas often remarked that he would be proud of such a rank. No thoughts for him of a belittling Private Hardy.

There was a mishap on the way back to Bovington Camp, Lawrence explained to Florence Hardy on 2 April 1924:

"I knew that on the parcel was the august name ... and so rather expected to hear of it. Partly it wasn't my fault. At my sedate riding-speed I passed a car (not a Car: just an ordinary four-wheeled passenger motor-propelled vehicle) not ostentatiously. A moment later it whistled past me, racing: and clung so to the centre of the road that it wasn't till the Weymouth cross-roads [Warmwell Cross, now a roundabout] that I could slip past: doing this time about two feet to its one. Till the car insulted me I'd been riding cautiously, feeling my parcel: but when I slowed down further on, & felt back, the carrier was empty.

"I turned round and rode back to Broadmayne, but found nothing. Today Mr Pattle (or Mrs probably) was kind to me, & I retied the thing with a piece of tow-rope, & got it safely to camp.

"The books are to be lent direct to people in the huts: the library lends them, but against deposit, & the fellows don't feel as free, to toss them about, as is desirable. So I'm going to plant them, singly, in deserving soil. After one has liked them they are assured of a wide lending.

"Palmer is well (too well, for my comfort: convalescence makes him the most exasperating little monkey of a man) but he has still got a heavy cold on him, & so he mustn't come to Max Gate. I'll take your kind invitation literally, & bring him over as soon as it is alright."

E. M. Forster had also been at Max Gate, Florence mentions in a letter to Sydney Cockerell on 11 April 1924, in which she displays total admiration for her favourite Colonel:

"Lawrence came to see us a fortnight ago, and is coming – I think – this Sunday. He is one of the few entirely satisfactory people in the world. He can be so very kind. He has influenza but looks well, and has a most powerful motor-cycle ... E. M. Forster came to see him ... He liked him greatly. It was their first meeting ..."

E. M. Forster and the Hardys drop in

On Friday 20 June 1924 E. M. Forster arrived at Clouds Hill to spend the weekend. "Probably it is out of pity, to cheer me up," Lawrence had written earlier in the week to Florence Hardy. "He would be shocked to know that I am pitying him, or rather his sojourn among the beetles & the rhododendron-bloom. Russell, Palmer & I will go up in turn to keep him company: but we seem slender fare for a real novelist. So I wondered if you and Mr Hardy could do anything."

Despite some reservations, they did call on 21 June. Earlier in the day, Mrs Hardy had written to Sydney Cockerell: "Lawrence came in last week, and seemed not well. He said he had broken a rib on the floor of his hut, which made motor-cycling a little difficult. So I should think. If T.H. will go we are intending to have tea with him at his cottage this afternoon – E. M. Forster being there. But I do not know whether T.H. will go. At all events the car is ordered and I am hoping for the best. E. M. Forster is a very good companion for Lawrence I think – he is so gentle and broad-minded, and more sympathetic, I think, than anyone I know."

Hardy was persuaded, and Forster recalled the afternoon in his article in The Listener. "I liked the place at once," he said. "His friends were friendly, I felt easy, and to feel easy was, in T.E.'s eyes a great recommendation." That sunny afternoon Thomas Hardy turned up, and "seemed to come on a visit to us all, and not specially his host. Thomas Hardy and Mrs Hardy came up the narrow stairway into the little brown room and there they were – guests to us all. To think of Clouds Hill as T.E.'s home is to get the wrong idea of it. It wasn't his home, it was rather his 'pied-a-terre', the place where his feet touched the ground for a moment and found rest."

Lawrence was delighted with his guests. "I needn't tell you how glad I was that Mr Hardy and yourself came to Clouds Hill the other day," he wrote to Florence Hardy. "A tremendous favour: and it makes me proud of the place."

He promised to return the call, to Dorchester on 1 July 1924 when the Balliol Players from Oxford were to perform *The Oresteia* as *The Curse of the House of Atreus* on the lawn at Max Gate. "I'll come over at 4.30 & if it is still going on, will hide in the bushes to hear the last act."

In the event there was no pair of blue eyes concealed in the bushes, to Florence's disappointment. A month later, on 31 July, Lawrence set out his excuses to her saying the Greek play "was a tragedy here as well as in the Orestes family. The Staff Sergt. knew I wanted to get off promptly from work, & so he put me on to job after job, from 3.30 onwards, till I was too late.

"This was his revenge for my having been clever a day or two before. The business was so sickening that I went away & had a feast of eggs & bacon, & pretended to be happy without spiritual food. The Staff Sergt. has had a bad life since, & is sorry. Says I can get off early any day I like: I don't like ... now."

The principal purpose of this letter was to set out, at length, the financial arrangements by which the selected subscribers could reserve their copies of the first edition of *Seven Pillars of Wisdom*. In effect he tried to solicit 30 guineas with half being payable immediately: "If you still require it you will have to send a cheque for fifteen guineas to my bank manager, Bank of Liverpool and Martin's, 68 Lombard Street, London E.C.3. Cheque payable to T. E .Lawrence, and marked 'Seven Pillars Acct.'." Which presumably they did as the first subscribers' edition of *Seven Pillars of Wisdom* would be listed as lot 248 in the sale of Hardy's library, on 26 May 1936. Another "of my copies of the first edition of T. E. Lawrence's *Seven Pillars of Wisdom*" Florence left to her friend Irene Cooper Willis when she died on 17 October 1937. She seems to have seen the subscriptions to the book as a chance to help Lawrence financially.

'Public Shaw' at Clouds Hill

Lawrence was becoming increasingly anxious to escape from Bovington Camp and the Royal Tank Corps. He had his chance to rejoin the Royal Air Force in May 1924 when Air Chief Marshal Sir Hugh Trenchard considered he would be the ideal person to write the official history of the Royal Flying Corps during the Great War. It emerged during discussions in London that this would be a three-year assignment and would give Lawrence officer status once more.

He turned the offer down, probably because he realised the application and strain, and the responsibility, that level of writing would demand.

In July 1924 George Bernard Shaw [1856–1950] sent a copy of his *Saint Joan of Arc*, published in 1923, to Lawrence at Bovington Camp. "Private Shaw from Public Shaw", it was inscribed. Lawrence was delighted with it, but eventually he loaned it around the camp and it was lost. A replacement was requested, similarly inscribed by its author: "To Pte. Shaw from Public Shaw."

That year Shaw visited Lawrence: "He came snuffing the air and taking stock of everything like a sergeant-major ... I really think he liked it."

15 August was the eve of Lawrence's thirty-sixth birthday and he was visited at Bovington Camp by Air Marshal Sir John Salmond, with his wife. They insisted upon taking him out for dinner. Lawrence told them he was fed up with Bovington and wanted to be allowed back into the R.A.F.

Salmond said he would see if he could prepare the ground; he would become Air Officer Commanding-in-Chief from 1 January 1925.

Distinguished guests to Glastonbury

Siegfried Sassoon and T. E. Lawrence were visitors to the Hardys at Max Gate on 6 August 1924 when they arranged a joint outing for later in the month. At Glastonbury, the composer Rutland Boughton [1878–1960] was producing an operatic version of Thomas Hardy's last play, *Iseult, or the Famous Tragedy of the Queen of Cornwall*. It was a project on a Wagnerian scale, with nationalistic musical dramas that seemed set to turn Glastonbury into the British Bayreuth.

Mr and Mrs Hardy drove across to hear the performance on 28 August

1924, apparently in the company of E. M. Forster, Siegfried Sassoon and T. E. Lawrence. Lawrence had left his motor-cycle at Dorchester. It was an evening that would go into Hardy folklore as the night when on his return to Max Gate Thomas Hardy pointedly removed the coal from the fire, to save it for another day. His maid, Nellie Titterington, had left a kettle boiling on the trivet for Lawrence's cup of Bovril. He then motor-cycled back to Clouds Hill.

Invited to edit Hardy's diary

1925 was the year Lawrence came closer to the Hardys, claiming to see them every Sunday and being invited by Florence to edit her husband's diary for publication. As with the R.A.F. history he allowed the matter to drop. He did however enjoy talking to Thomas on matters of life and death and literature. He notes that once they were discussing a translation of La Fontaine's *Fables* when an "old hen" butted in and by the time she stopped jawing Thomas had forgotten ever reading the book.

It was excusable. Hardy was now aged 85.

"The truth is," wrote Lawrence, "that a film seems to slip over his mind at times now: and the present is then obscured by events of his childhood. He talked next of seeing Scots Greys in a public-house in Dorchester drinking strong ale, whose fumes made him (aet. 6) drunken."

For all that, signs of advancing years notwithstanding, Lawrence admired the country's leading novelist immensely:

"And the standards of the man! He feels interest in everyone, and veneration for no-one. I've not found in him any bowing-down, moral or material or spiritual."

Back into the R.A.F.

Lawrence was now becoming desperate to leave Bovington Camp. On 6 February 1925 he wrote to Air Chief Marshal Sir Hugh Trenchard formally asking to be allowed to transfer from the Royal Tank Corps back into the Royal Air Force.

In May 1925 Lawrence was told that his request had been rejected. Undisuaded, he moved on to use his political influence by seeing John Buchan, who had been the Director of Information at the end of the Great War, and talked him into raising the matter with the Prime Minister, Stanley Baldwin.

Lawrence did not hesitate to use his trump card. There was one ultimate weapon of emotional blackmail; that either he had his own way or he would take his life. No one wanted to go down in history as the officer whose sole remembered contribution to his country's annals was that he had brought about the suicide of the national hero.

His suicide threat was made to Edward Garnett on 13 June 1925: "Trenchard withdrew his objection to my rejoining the Air Force. I got seventh-heaven for two weeks: but then Sam Hoare [Secretary of State for Air] came back from Mespot [Mesopotamia, now Iraq] and refused to entertain the idea. That, and the closer acquaintance with *The Seven Pillars* (which I now know better than anyone ever will) have together convinced me that I'm no bloody good on earth. So I'm going to quit: but in my usual comic fashion I'm going to finish the reprint and square up with Cape before I hop it. There is nothing like deliberation, order and regularity in these things.

"I shall bequeath my notes on life in the recruits camp of the R.A.F. [his manuscript of *The Mint*]. They will disappoint you.

Garnett relayed the threat to George Bernard Shaw who warned Prime Minister Stanley Baldwin of the "possibility of an appalling scandal, especially after Lowell Thomas's book". This was *With Lawrence in Arabia* which had given a fresh boost to the Lawrence legend.

On 1 July 1925 Lawrence visited Air Chief Marshal Sir Hugh Trenchard, the Chief of Air Staff, to be told that, against his better judgement, Trenchard would submit to Lawrence's infuriatingly persistent demands and accept his transfer from the Tank Corps to the Royal Air Force. Lawrence was elated; he threw his Brough Superior "Boanerges" at the tarmac, claiming a record 108 m.p.h. on his return to Bovington Camp.

On 3 November 1925, after the blackmail had worked and he was at Cranwell, Lawrence made the point to Francis Rodd that it had been no idle whim: "Mark me down for a further spell of quite happy existence. That also is an odd change, for I had made up my mind, in Bovington, to come to a natural end about Xmas, when the reprint of my book would have been finished."

Stanley Baldwin would instead be the toast of that Christmas, as Lawrence recalled in a letter to John Buchan on 26 December 1928: "I wanted you to know I'm making the best use I can of the gift you led Mr Baldwin into giving me in 1925." Lawrence obtained a posting to romantic parts, to northern India where the Royal Air Force had several squadrons of Bristol Fighters and some flights of bombers.

Abandoned Bovington manuscripts: 'burning money'

When Lawrence prepared to leave Dorset for India in November 1926 he is said to have abandoned several tea-chests full of manuscripts. They were in a tiny room at Woodside Cottage, a wooden bungalow a quarter of a mile from the Military Hospital, on the outskirts of Bovington Camp. Lawrence and Corporal Alec Dixon rented the room from the camp hairdresser, J. Forse.

The pair used the room late at night when their day's duties were over and were said to study by the light of a candle or oil-lamp into the early hours. The room was used intensively for about twelve months, Mr Forse recalled:

"They both seemed to me to be mysterious men, and both spent the best part of the nights in the little room writing.

"Then they both left hurriedly. They simply brought back the keys and said they were very sorry they had to go away. There was a mass of literature in the room, and they asked if I would clear it up and dispose of it by burning the stuff.

"I casually looked through any amount of it and there were drawings and reams of handwritten manuscript. Instead of burning it I packed it in boxes. Then later my father, Mr J. W. Forse, a picture-framer, of Church Passage, Weymouth, who is rather interested in literature, recognised, as I did, that there was a lot of interesting material there besides the sketches.

"He took it to Weymouth to look it through.

"Although Lawrence and Dixon were both literary men, I don't think they were collaborators. They merely worked together because they were friends and they were both interested in writing.

"Dixon wrote a lot for magazines, and he was clever with his pen, but I am convinced that some of the sketches were Lawrence's own work."

Mr Forse opened an illustrated copy of Lowell Thomas's *With Lawrence in Arabia* and pointed out two drawings which he recognised as having been among the literature he found in the room. One was a well-known drawing of Lawrence himself in Arabian dress, and the other showed a desert scene of a train of camels on a journey.

"From the notes and manuscripts I saw after they had gone I am more than convinced that the whole of *Seven Pillars of Wisdom* was written in the little room here," continued Mr Forse.

"A great quantity of manuscript left behind was, of course, burned. We had a bonfire in the garden with some of it. There were three or four tea chests full. In those days the men were merely Private Shaw and Corporal Dixon, but I realise now I was burning money.

"Lawrence left behind a lion skin which he loved. He gave it to me and we destroyed it just the other day. He also left the chair in which he used to sit and work. It was a plain one which he made himself. We converted it into a small dressing-table which we now use in one of the bedrooms."

After Lawrence had died in 1935, a Dorset County Chronicle reporter called on J. W. Forse in Weymouth who embarked upon a search for the boxes of odds and ends he thought he had kept. In particular he remembered a sketch of a black-visaged Arab rider in flowing robes. Some of the manuscripts had apparently been given to a young girl working in Forse's shop, Miss Read, and it was assumed they were still in her possession.

Reflections from Karachi on Wessex and Hardy

Lawrence packed his copies of the Bible, *War and Peace*, and Samuel Pepys's Diaries for his passage to India. He sailed from Southampton on 7 December 1926 in the troopship *Derbyshire*. His most vivid description of the voyage concerns the women's latrines. He watched these being unblocked by hand as the Orderly Officer pulled out "a most white bundle" of sanitary towels.

His posting was to the Aircraft Depôt at Drigh Road, Karachi, in the high, dry arid lands of India's North-West Frontier District. That would remind him of the opposite end of the same desert, the Sinai, and the letters from Dorset made him homesick. From Florence Hardy came the news that Thomas Hardy's beloved rough-haired terrier, Wessex – who had not only bitten the postman but had gone on to notch up John Galsworthy – had to be put down with a tumour at the age of thirteen on 27 December 1926.

"Wessex was a terror," Nellie Titterington of the Max Gate staff would recall. "No guest could pick up a spoon or anything dropped without the probability of a nasty nip on the hand. T.H. could do anything with the dog without danger, while if the dog was in a good mood, Mrs Hardy could sometimes pick up a dropped object safely. Colonel Lawrence ... was the only other person who could safely deal with Wessex: he could pick up anything without ill humour on its part.

"Wessex was very fond of T.E.L. who would pat him and speak to him and had a wonderful power over him. To understand what a remarkable influence Lawrence had on this dog it must be remembered that no one, with, as I say, the sole exception of T.H. himself, could or would dare touch, or go near, him without the probability of a snap or a bite: he was a fierce, ugly-tempered beast."

Wessex was a strange dog. Hardy was positive the terrier could sense that William Watkins, the founder of the Society of Dorset Men in London, was dying as the two men chatted at Max Gate. Wessex had sniffed Watkins's trousers and rushed from the room with a prolonged howl. He dashed riotously up and down the stairs and was released into the garden where he searched for an unfindable marauder. At 10 p.m. on 18 April 1925 Watkins left Max Gate for his Dorchester hotel room, and the grim reaper followed. Watkins died in his sleep at midnight.

Lawrence heard about the canine premonition. "I'm not surprised," he said. "There is an Arab proverb: 'The dog sees the Angel of Death first.' That is what he saw."

For Wessex there would be a special stone from Thomas Hardy in the pets' cemetery at Max Gate: "Wessex – Faithful and Unflinching."

Lawrence's first comment to Florence Hardy in response to the news, from Karachi on 11 January 1927, concerned another odd piece of behaviour, Lawrence's own, which had puzzled the Hardys. It was the manner of his parting from Max Gate on what would turn out to be the last occasion when he saw Thomas Hardy:

"It was my doing. The afternoon was raw and miserable, like the day, and when T.H. turned back into the house to get a shawl (as I guessed) instantly I ran the bicycle out into the road and away, so that no possible reproach might lie against me for having helped him into the danger of a chill.

"The knowing you and having the freedom of Max Gate has been a delightful privilege for nearly four years. I cannot tell you how grateful I am to you both: and how much I look forward to finding you there when I come back. Eighty-six is nothing of an age, so long as its bearer is not content with it; in fact it is still fourteen years short of a decent score in cricket.

"I hope Wessex had a peaceful parting. The killing of animals just because they are ill or old is not a medicine we apply to our own species.

"Karachi feels inordinately far away from every interest I ever had. However it will pass."

On 10 March 1927 in London, Jonathan Cape published the shorter public version of *Seven Pillars of Wisdom*, under the less weighty title of *Revolt in the Desert*. The Lawrence legend was hardly disappearing. By 5 May Lawrence had word of his return to fame, and wrote to Florence Hardy: "The Cape abridgement is selling like ripe apples, they tell me. I hate that little book.

"My restlessness, on first seeing Karachi, has faded. I keep myself strictly to camp, and make time pass easily enough with books, reading and re-reading the old things I have read and liked, but not treated ceremoniously enough, in my youth."

As with many of his letters to Florence he had to start with excuses. This time it was an apology for waiting three months before replying to her answer to his January letter.

Then he returned to writing what amounts to Wessex's obituary, realising it would please Thomas and to offset any offence caused by earlier remarks, such as those about animals making him feel uncomfortable. Wessex, he now made clear, was the exception:

"The death of Wessex is a loss to me. He was so firm and decisive a being: one who always knew his own mind, and never hesitated to change it, if he thought fit.

"So doing he showed a very healthy disregard for the feelings of merely temporary visitors. Few dogs appeal to me: but Wessex gained my very definite respect. And the poor beast (after I felt towards him) changed his tone & became very kind. Max Gate will not seem quite right now. He must be a very great loss to you and T.H. I'm so sorry: I hope you and T.H. are otherwise well."

He knew, however, that the odds were lengthening against Thomas Hardy reaching the ninetieth birthday he had set his mind upon. Max Gate, he realised, would soon be lacking more than poor Wessex. He wrote to Sydney

Cockerell on 27 May 1927 about Hardy's next immediate objective, his eighty-seventh birthday: "I shall be with you in spirit on the lawn at Max Gate in July. In a week it will be his birthday. I keep on hoping he will be alive (and not a burden to himself) in 1931 when I'm due back.

"It is selfish to want old people to go on outliving their health & strength: but somehow T.H. is different. I'd like his head to exist for ever, like the head and arms of G.B.S. They are supreme works of art."

The admiration was mutual, at least as far as Florence Hardy was concerned. She wrote to Robert Graves on 13 June 1927: "I consider him the most marvellous human being I have ever met. It is not his exploits in Arabia that attract me, nor the fact he is a celebrity: it is his character that is so splendid."

For Lawrence, in his fortieth year, there was the onset of life's health problems. His hearing had become somewhat impaired and his staring blue eyes were upset by the intensity of Karachi light. They were particularly strained by reading.

On 30 August 1927 the public person with the best-selling *Revolt in the Desert* to his name, Colonel Thomas Edward Lawrence of Arabia, legally became Aircraftman Thomas Edward Shaw, as his private person was changed by deed poll. The name had first been assumed, as Private Shaw, on entry to the Tank Corps at Bovington in 1923. Note that despite what other authors seem to think, there is no 's' in the middle of his R.A.F. rank; Aircraftman was just what it says – Aircraft-man.

Perhaps Lawrence felt safer drawing attention to himself while out of the country, but there will be the inevitable speculation that he is engaged in secret service operations in Afghanistan. The country has pacts with both Russia and Britain. Whilst Lawrence is in the sub-continent, the Amir of Afghanistan, Amanullah Khan, makes an official visit to Britain and is shown the tanks at Bovington and Lulworth on 20 March 1928.

For Lawrence, however, there is other news from Dorset.

An era came to a close in Dorchester at nine o'clock in the evening of 11 January 1928. The last words that Thomas Hardy would hear had been as it grew dark and Florence read to him from the *Rubáiyát of Omar Khayyám*.

When Lawrence was in Karachi his mother called at the Dorset cottage. She approved, and Lawrence wrote to her on 12 August 1927 with his further plans for it:

"I'm glad you liked Clouds Hill. Of course the cottage has been much changed since I left it. But if ever I get it again I'll soon put it right. The upstairs room is only half-finished. It will some day be as good as its wonderful situation deserves.

"That heath country is the most beautiful I've seen, & the rhododendrons in Moreton Park climb up the oak trees, like creepers, & hang 50 feet in the air, in showers of blossom.

Throw-away thoughts on the late Thomas Hardy

Lawrence's reflections on the death of Thomas Hardy are contained in his letter to Sydney Cockerell, from Karachi, on 2 February 1928.

"I feel very much for Mrs Hardy who remains like a plant which had grown up in a pot, from which the pot is suddenly stripped. She will find it hard to begin life again, [for] the third time. For T.H. none of us can have great regrets. His life was a triumph, just because it was prolonged for that last, unexpected, twenty years ... I could die, I hope, willingly, as T.H. would die ..."

He goes on to confirm that he has no more literary aspirations: "My writing is bad: and I'll do no more of it. Agreed that however bad it was the public would buy it, if signed: look at the publicity I've had. But I'd rather starve than be fed that way. Moral prostitution; nothing else ..."

Lawrence wrote again to Cockerell, who was Hardy's literary executor, on 22 February. In this letter, also from Karachi, he gives Cockerell carte blanche to censor the leavings of Thomas Hardy, author and poet, by destroying anything he finds which fails to reach his own standards:

"It is very good of you to have kept me so in touch with the passing of the great man. I'm touched that he should have put my bust on his wall. It has there kept better company than any other photo of mine has done ...

"I wonder if there was stuff he kept back for any reason except that of insufficient goodness. However you are safe to destroy anything of his which does not come up to your standard and his. He was so generously large a poet that his individual lines are of small value ..." It is with such literally throw-away remarks that Lawrence reveals more of himself than the subjects on which he is writing.

In a letter to William Rothenstein, the artist [1872–1945], he denies being a friend of Thomas Hardy:

"Not that I could be a friend of his: the difference in size and age and performance between us was too overwhelming: but because I'd seen a good deal of him, and he was so by himself, so characteristic a man, that each contact with him was an experience. I went each time, nervously: and came away gladly, saying 'It's all right'."

To Rothenstein, Lawrence also fumed at the way Dorchester's clergymen ("black-suited apes") had constantly tried to reclaim Hardy as spiritually one of their own:

"I regret Hardy's funeral. So little of it suited the old man's nature. He would have smiled, tolerantly, at it all: but I grow indignant for him, knowing that those sleek Deans and Canons were acting a lie behind his name. Hardy was too great to be suffered as an enemy of their faith: so he must be redeemed. Each birthday the Dorchester clergymen would insert a paragraph telling how his choir had carolled to the old man 'his favourite hymn'. He was mild and let himself be badgered, out of local loyalty. 'Which hymn would you like for tomorrow Mr Hardy?' 'Number 123' he'd snap back, wearied of all the nonsense: and that would be his favourite of the year, in next day's 'Gazette'.

"I wish these black-suited apes could once see the light with which they shine."

Then Lawrence makes a telling remark to Rothenstein about the three eminent men of letters of the age. He mentions that George Bernard Shaw is sitting for Rothenstein, for his portrait, and adds: "He is beclouded, like Hardy and Kipling, with works which tend to live more intensely than their creator ..." Here Lawrence, one feels, is excepting himself. There was one literary genius who was not an uninteresting personality; the press would concur.

Lawrence had these consoling thoughts for Hardy's widow, Florence, who continued to correspond with him after Thomas had died:

"You say you have failed him at every turn. Of course he did: everybody did. He was T.H. and if you'd met him or sufficed him at every turn you'd have been as good as T.H., which is absurd; though perhaps some people might think it should be put happier than that. But you know my feeling (worth something perhaps, because I've met so many thousands of what are esteemed great men) that T.H. was above and beyond all men living, as a person."

Such consolation was offset by Lawrence's opinions on what might be done with the house itself, to an extent that irritated Mrs Hardy: "T. E. Lawrence suggested that I leave Max Gate to some broken-down poet. But it really seems a part of my husband. His cat is lying within a few inches of my pen as I write, as he always does." Florence continued to live at Max Gate, surviving Thomas for ten years.

'The arch-spy of the world'

Accusations implicating Lawrence with a spying mission in India's troubled North-West Frontier District became uncontrollable after 5 December 1928 when he was at the border station of Miranshah in Wazirstan. The Daily News reported: "It is inferred he intends to move into Afghanistan." Miranshah had twenty-six R.A.F. officers and men, with 700 Indian scouts to guard them in a fort ringed by barbed wire, machine gun posts and searchlights. Lawrence showed no interest whatever in Indian history or culture and spent most of his free time listening to the gramophone or writing letters. One contains a beautiful description of the scenery: "Round us, a few miles off, in a ring are low bare porcelain-coloured hills, with chipped edges and a broken-bottle skyline. Afghanistan is 10 miles off."

An airman said Lawrence was learning Pushtu, from which the espionage inference was drawn, but Lawrence claimed it was a Greek lexicon he was using, in the process of translating Homer's *Odyssey*, at the Royal Air Force station of Miranshah where he was ostensibly working as a clerk. Not that the British United Press believed him.

Their story on the wires at the start of January was that Colonel T. E. Lawrence was "the arch-spy of the world". He was allegedly training groups of guerillas, which in the 1920s were slipping across the border from British territory much as their descendants would be doing from the same valleys in Pakistan in the 1980s. The agency's claims went into print in the Daily Herald, London, on 5 January 1929:

"Photographs supposed to be of Colonel Lawrence have been secretly procured from India, and distributed among the Afghan commanders, it is stated. If this be true – though in well informed London circles it is received with reserve – Lawrence of Arabia is maintaining his reputation as one of the most startling persons in the world.

"For some time his movements, as chronicled, have been mysterious, and a few months ago it was stated that he was in Afghanistan on a secret mission, though earlier in the same week it had been reported that he was in Amritsar, posing as a Mohammedan saint."

Two days later there were the denials, quoting the official Amany Afghan newspaper of Kabul as considering Lawrence's role to be exaggerated:

"We do not believe in Colonel Lawrence's power and skill. He is only an Englishman."

Either way, the game was up. Send him home, the Air Ministry ordered. Lawrence docked at Plymouth on 2 February 1929, from the steamship *Rajputuna*. He received VIP treatment, which did nothing to allay press suspicions – met by a naval tender he was whisked through customs to a meal with the Royal Navy's Commander-in-Chief Plymouth. Met by reporters off the train at Paddington Lawrence gave the press all they needed by saying: "I am Mr Smith." He later resumed his Dorset contacts. In particular, at Whitsun, he visited Thomas Hardy's widow, Florence, at Max Gate. He also wrote to R. D. Blumenfeld, the editor of the Daily Express:

"I got ticked off by the Air Ministry, and told that I'd get the sack if I saw any more newspaper people – so since this I've been sort of paralysed. Thank heaven the subject has blown over for the present. I wonder what the next spasm will be about."

New Brough and buys Clouds Hill

By 19 March 1929 he was very much at home, and delighting in the fact in a letter to his mother: "I saw Clouds Hill. It is as lovely as ever."

Bernard and Charlotte Shaw arranged for Lawrence to be sent, anonymously, the Brough Superior motor-cycle registration UL 656 which he named "George VI" – the numbers had gone yearly in succession from George I in 1923. This one might otherwise be quite a premonition for 1929, in that the succession would eventually go to George, Duke of York, after its brief spell with Edward, Prince of Wales. In March 1929 he arrived on it at Cattewater Air Station, Plymouth (the purpose of which was summed up by its telegraphic address, "Aeronautics, Plymouth"), which was about to be renamed Mount Batten.

He was in the process of buying the freehold of the Clouds Hill cottage, he told his mother on 19 March 1929: "I have paid for it now: only the conveyance is not yet ready. Four years has that wretched land agent been bungling his business. My job here is going to be given me in about 10 days or so. Till then I just busy myself doing some typing work in an office, helping a clerk who is too full of work."

On 27 April 1929 Lawrence wrote from Cattewater to Jock Chambers who had been an aircraft-hand at Farnborough: "Clouds Hill is still there. I saw it for an hour in February. It is as lovely as ever: only the chimney-pots are added as a monument to the new tenants' taste. Jock, the old tenants were 'some' people.

"You and me, & Guy, of the R.A.F. and the brothers Salmond (Marshals of sorts) [Air Chief Marshal Sir Geoffrey Salmond and Air Marshal Sir John Salmond], Hardy, Graves, Siegfried Sassoon, poets: Forster, Tomlinson, Garnett, prose-writers. Spencer and John, artists. It was a good place while it lasted. I wish there was a Clouds Hill in every camp, assigned for the use of aircraft hands."

Lawrence had been told Chambers was dead but succeeded in tracing him to a G.P.O. sorting office.

On May Day in 1929 Lawrence wrote to his mother from Plymouth about the cottage at Clouds Hill, its impending purchase – for some reason still delayed – and an Essex land-sale which is to bring "only about £4,000". This was the disposal of five acres at Pole Hill, Chingford, which he had bought on 1 September 1919 and built a house.

"By all means take some of the rhododendrons from Clouds Hill. There are only too many of them. I had hoped to put in some red and some white ones, to mix up the colour: and a lot of magnolias, which carry beautiful great flowers. There seems to be some hitch over the purchase. I've given them a week to say yes or no. Tired of waiting, I am.

"Epping Forest want Pole Hill, to add to the forest. I'm likely to agree to that, as it would be a crime to build streets over it. Only, of course, it means I won't get much money for it: perhaps only about £4,000. Its real value is as building land, for which I don't wish to sell it. However, it will be months before they settle anything.

"I've only been three times out of camp since I've been here: twice to London for a few hours, and last week to Plymouth, to eat a meal, with Lady

T.E.Shaw on
Brough Superior motor-cycles
RK 4907 and UL 656:
looking up from the
latter at its
manufacturer, George Brough.

[Nancy] Astor, who came here and looked me up. I like her: though she is tiring. If you go to Clouds Hill, see Sergt. Knowles, who will help you, if you want any help.

"Your Inverness clock is in his cupboard, for dryness sake. I've told Lionel Curtis [colonial scholar] he may use the cottage, for week-ends, if he likes. The tenants have gone. It is not damaged. The last time I was in London I met Arnie [brother Arnold], late at night, near Russell Square. He knew me, & told me about his book. G.B.S. [Shaw] is in the Adriatic, on an island.

"If you see [E.T.] Leeds again, tell him I will not be able to come to Oxford till after September, after his Schneider Cup Race. They have set me on to do some of the clerical work for that."

Lawrence would become the freehold owner of the Dorset cottage and its banks of rhododendron in 1929. He bought Clouds Hill from Henry Rupert Fetherstonhaugh Frampton [1861–1955] of Moreton House for £450.

Despite his deed-poll name change to Shaw, he used the Thomas Edward Ross name in which he had been renting the cottage.

The deal had been completed but without the ground opposite, which Lawrence also intended buying, as he would explain to his mother on 25 April 1931:

"The estate would not sell the opposite side of the road – but might give me a long lease of it. Knowles' lease runs out in 3 years or so. I want to prevent other bungalows from springing up opposite my patch. It takes the estate months to make up its mind!"

In 1929 a copy of D. H. Lawrence's *Lady Chatterley's Lover* appeared in Lawrence's (no relation) locker at Cattewater, sent by Edward Marsh to whom T.E.L. would write on 18 April 1929: "I'm re-reading it with a slow deliberate carelessness: going to fancy that I've never read a D.H.L. before, and that it's up to me to appraise this new man and manner. D.H.L. has always been so rich and ripe a writer to me, before, that I'm deeply puzzled and hurt by this *Lady Chatterley* of his.

"Surely the sex business isn't worth all this damned fuss? I've met only a handful of people who really cared a biscuit for it."

Bill Bugg: the friend who wouldn't talk

One of Lawrence's Bovington friends at this time was Bill Bugg who was the proprietor of the camp's Garrison Cinema. His wife miscarried their first child after an over-exuberant soldier fired a starting pistol during a cowboy film.

Bill Bugg seems to have the Clouds Hill handyman; he would construct Lawrence's swimming pool in 1933. I tracked him down in 1968 to his terraced town house opposite the White Hart Hotel at the bottom end of High East Street in Dorchester, but he was unforthcoming as my contemporary memo about the doorstep-meeting records:

"B.B. claimed to have known Lawrence more or less from the time he first went to Bovington and also claimed to have been the last person to see Lawrence alive. B.B. did work for Lawrence on and off and they also had private correspondence. He's got a large number of letters from Lawrence but feels that they should always remain private. He feels that Lawrence himself would have wanted it that way and says that if he had published anything while Lawrence was alive, Lawrence would have regarded it as a betrayal and he would have lost his friendship. He doesn't see that his death makes any difference. He still regards it as wrong to do anything that might bring publicity to Lawrence.

"When I first spoke to B.B. he was very friendly, very helpful, and said I was to return the next day and he was more than prepared to chat to me. When I arrived this morning [the next day] he was a totally different man. He refused to have anything on tape, even the most harmless recollections. He didn't want to speak to me, kept wanting to stop the conversation and generally gave me the impression of knowing too much, in fact far too much.

"He is now aged about 75, and was known to Lawrence as B.B. During the whole brief course of the talk he kept wanting to know what I was getting at and he was afraid that his information might be used to smear Lawrence. I told him that I was primarily interested in anything he could tell me about Lawrence's death and he replied that he knew quite a lot that would interest me but that it was information which he has no intention of telling anyone."

Choosing the sculptor for Hardy's memorial

In 1929 the issue was raised of who should be commissioned for a sculpture of Thomas Hardy. Lawrence wrote to Sydney Cockerell, from Plymouth, on 29 July 1929 and demolished Jacob Epstein's credentials:

"Epstein is the obvious choice, only he is not, I expect, a Hardy lover, and when he improvises he is not enchanting ... it is embarrassing to have four good English sculptors ..." Of these, following Lawrence's advice, the bronze that sits at the Top o' Town, Dorchester, is the work of Eric Kennington, the illustrator for the *Seven Pillars of Wisdom*. He would in turn carve Lawrence's effigy for St Martin's church in Wareham.

Meantime, on the subject of Dorchester's new-found interest in the late great Thomas Hardy – whom it ignored for most of his lifetime, until the Prince of Wales made the pilgrimage to see the old man at Max Gate – Lawrence is scathing about the town: "Too late, poor things. He has assumed half Wessex for his own."

Speed-boats on Southampton Water

Lawrence's next interlude from Dorset was much nearer home and on another edge of the same great tract of heathland, on the eastern side of the New Forest. He worked in Southampton Water on the prototype high-speed launches which the Royal Air Force needed as target-towing and air-sea rescue craft. In terms of Lawrence's quick pace career it was to be a relatively long assignment. As Aircraftman 338171 Shaw, on Southampton Water with the use of a fast launch, Lawrence helped to manage the Schneider Cup sea-plane races over the Solent in 1929.

There he fell out with the Minister for Air in the new Labour Government, Lord Thomson, or rather came a little too close to him.

Thomson asked this British aircraftman why he was sweeping the slipway for the Italian competitors. It was a stupid question to ask and came from a naive politician who was incensed when a photograph of the moment was snapped by one of the Lawrence watchers. Such is the legend, that it appeared in newspapers across the globe, and Thomson all but had Lawrence thrown out of the service, but no one seems to have traced a single contemporary version of the story.

Lawrence kept a low profile until, at 11.30 a.m. on 4 February 1931, back at the seaplane base in Plymouth Sound which was now called Mount Batten, he watched his commanding officer, Wing-Commander Charles Tucker, take himself and eight other men to their deaths. They were in Blackburn Irish flying-boat S238 which Tucker had brought down in a steep dive. Lawrence told the inquest:

"Then she struck the water just under the pilot's seat, forward near the

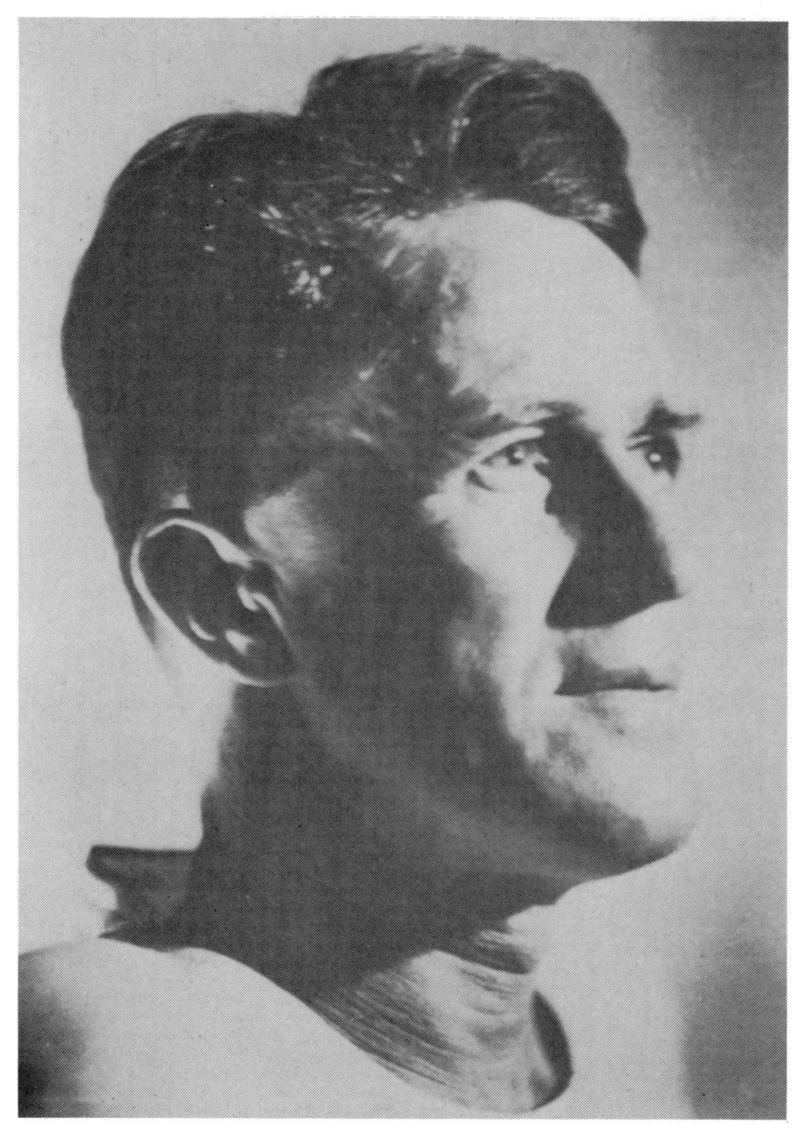

Lawrence in 1931: at 43, photographed by Howard Costa.

bow. The tail of the machine came left, her main planes crashed into the water and folded back altogether. The hull dived straight down to the bottom." Asked if he would have flown with Tucker, Lawrence replied: "only if I had been ordered to do so."

Lawrence used his influence with Nancy Astor, who as Lady Astor was the Member of Parliament for Plymouth, to ensure that there was never again a case in which an officer pulled rank, as Tucker had done, to take command from the pilot. Tucker was experienced in the air, but not in landing on water.

Lawrence was inspired by this incident into a practical crusade to provide the Royal Air Force with fast purpose-built launches that could reach crash sites in less than half the time taken by their standard Navy-type craft.

He returned to Southampton Water, to the British Power Boat Company at Hythe, to give the Royal Air Force its own first generation of high-speed launches. Lawrence spent more time in the water on the prototypes than anyone and continually returned with suggestions for further improvements. By mid-1931 he had completed the most precise piece of writing of his life – hailed by David Garnett as "a masterpiece of technology" – the 80 foolscap pages of *Notes on Handling the 200 Class Seaplane Tender.*

As with Afghanistan, however, the press became increasingly interested and on 22 October 1932 Lawrence wrote to Arthur Hall:

"Motor-boat building is all over. A Sunday newspaper blew upon that, with headlines that said more than the truth (imagine, can you, a headline that said less ... my mind boggles at it!). So the Air Ministry chased me quickly out of that job, and out of my lodgings at Hythe."

Heath-fires to prolonged frosts

"F.E.H. from T.E.S." was Lawrence's inscription in the copy of *Odyssey of Homer* which he sent to Florence Hardy as her "kind of heavy Christmas card" on 15 December 1932. Her thank you letter found him languishing miserably in Plymouth. He replied from there on 9 January 1933: "Your letter came while I was away and then I got rather out of sorts. So for a week or more I have not written a line to anybody. I am glad you like the *Odyssey* for what it is ...

"Of course original work is better, but I have no mind for that: and if to move me takes a cataclysm as big as the war, then I hope I'll write no more! Your offer about shelves [offering her carpenter] is very good: but you would defeat the object of those five years of work. The *Odyssey* must provide the finishing of my cottage ... It's rather amusing, being suddenly rich ..."

On 7 February 1933 George Bernard Shaw posted Lawrence a third copy of his *Saint Joan of Arc.* The previous two were borrowed but not returned. "Hence this third copy," Lawrence wrote, "with its pessimistic inscription." Shaw's words were amusing, actually: "To Shaw from Shaw to replace many stolen copies until this, too, is stolen."

In the spring Mrs Hardy dropped by, after sending a note of her intention which Lawrence passed to Mrs Knowles, knowing that he was away but hoping to see the flora performing. She was being a little premature, Lawrence told her from Plymouth on 25 April 1933: "The flowers do not yet come to much. The laurel has been wonderful, this spring: better than ever I have seen it, and very scented; but you are too soon for the rhododendrons. Only two of mine, and your Thomas Hardy-Eden Phillpotts one [a cultivar] have bloomed as yet. Yours is quite picking up now, with about 20 good flowers: but it takes hundreds of plants to make a show on the hill-side and for that we must wait for the Pontica [common purple sort] to come out.

They are full of bud, but not yet showing colour."

He then mentions his mother, Sarah, and elder brother, Bob, "still stuck half-way up their river" in China when he last heard from that branch of the family in mid-February, and is disparaging about her efforts to prettify Clouds Hill: "My mother must have put in dozens of daffodils and things, garden flowers, near the house, for the whole of my little patch of grass has been full of them. I am afraid I thought them out of place. They spoiled the picture. However the rabbits seem to like them, and I have offered Mrs Knowles the rest. Clouds Hill is no place for tame flowers."

Lawrence was becoming something of a stranger to the place, travelling to Suffolk in April, the Isle of Wight in May, having lodgings in the Southampton suburbs from July, but he returned briefly to Clouds Hill on 24 September 1933.

Lawrence wrote to his mother about the cottage, from Southampton the following day:

"I was there yesterday, for the evening, and lit its first fire in the book-rom. No smoke, and little smell of smoke upstairs: while the draught seemed plenty. In fact it burned very brightly, and I enjoyed it for the night was wet, like my clothes.

"Not much progress in the public works. The ram is not yet satisfactory, but is being improved. The heating apparatus is at last definitely ordered. Upstairs is due for its second anti-wood-worm poisoning, and stripped bare for the operation. The bathroom is not yet cemented-round, and the bath waits in the garage for the boiler to be first installed.

"The book-room is all finished except for its fender, which I have not yet designed. My books fill one of the two shelved walls; the one on which the dishes used to sit north side. The opposite wall waits with empty shelves. Only a remnant of my books have survived their ten year exile: but all the Kelmscotts are present in good order ...

"The book-room window has two fixed side-panels, cemented into the stone frame, and a pivoting centre-pane, in a stainless steel frame. That gives enough light and air to suit me.

"The other furniture is the window-seat, an affair six feet each way, built up of Bob's former bed and a big box-spring mattress: very comfortable and useful. I propose to move Mrs. Hardy's little stool down there, as a table; and the fender will complete it. What used to be the bed-room, upstairs, I am turning into a work-room, to hold a table and papers and ink and food and probably the gramophone and my clothes. That will make the upstairs sitting-room big enough to walk about in.

"The staircase has been sheathed in oak three-ply: and the Spencer landscape panelled into the gable, quite successfully. With the finishing of the bath-room, I will have the workmen out of it, and the whole house finished, except for what is reserved for my own hands.

"The last five months of autumn were wild with heath-fires. One would have burned me out, but for the fire-bank and the Tank Corps. It has killed many of those promising young firs between me and the sentry-box on the road at the top of the hill. Gallows Hill is utterly laid waste, and whole miles of heath and wood between Wool and Wareham. As for the New Forest, not for 40 years has so much been damaged. However the late rains have stopped all fear.

"I have asked Mrs Knowles to take all the border plants she can, as my wall-footing operations in the next stage of repair will interfere with them."

Lawrence wrote again to his mother on 27 September 1933, and makes it clear he can cope with no more rhododendrons. It had been a summer of drought and heath-fires, and the Clouds Hill jungle was under threat:

"I cannot manage any more rhododendrons this autumn, for all my money has gone on the changes to the cottage. To finish the water and heating business I will probably have to anticipate my next payment of American royalties on the *Odyssey*. Until it is all finished I cannot say exactly what will be the total cost – more than I had expected, but then I have done more than I meant. Improvements suggest themselves, and it was now or never to put them in. So I have plunged, rather. All bills are paid, to date, but little remains.

"Another reason against more rhododendrons is space – or the lack of it. The shrubs are growing like wild-fire, and it is becoming increasingly difficult to force a way between them.

"Before new ones can be put in, the wild ones must be cut back: and that I shall have no time to do before I am living there. I get to the cottage only for a few hours a fortnight: hardly ever for a night.

"The place needs living in, badly. I would like to find a tenant for the winter, but cannot well offer it, without kitchen or bedroom: and will the water-works be finished? They are so slow, these firms. Even the ram is left undone, half-working and half anyhow.

"Mrs Knowles has voted against more apple-trees, because some soldiers raided her garden this summer and stole all her fruit before it was even ripe. The trees bore a heavy and splendid crop. She is pleased with the quarter of the garden that has been wired and dug. Many potatoes, I gather.

"Brian is in London and Pat at Clouds Hill. He has cut a lot of wood for her & me: but she does not let him help her in the garden. I have got Billy Bray [Bugg, according to what he told me in 1968] to give Pat jobs in my public works – water, bricklaying, cementing: and plan more for him. The fire risks this year have been really bad, and before next summer I shall have taken real precautions against the danger. Pat can do most of them for us. The Knowles family is queer. They get on best apart. Pat usually lives in my cottage, but feeds with Mrs Knowles ...

"I have not yet cleared in my own mind the design of a fender for the book-room. The stainless steel top of the upstairs one is a complete success. The seat of the new one must be stainless too.

"Your cheque for £50 came early in August and I wrote to thank you for it. It went on the cottage, of course, with my *Odyssey* money. I still have some in hand, but not quite enough, I expect. However next month more comes from the States. So please do not bother yourself to send more. It is never hard for me to make money – a rare and fortunate state that I try not to abuse!

"Our marvellous summer has definitely broken. We have had two weeks of very unsettled weather. High time too, with these droughts and heath-fires all over England."

On 5 November, in the next letter to his mother in China, Lawrence explains in detail the cost and practicalities of the installation of the water-works:

"The cottage is not finished. The boiler and bath are in course of installation, but will take quite two weeks more. I shall be so glad to have it to myself, after they finish. The works have dragged on all summer. Just now I am employing Pat and young Way & Cooper to dig a great water-tank in the ground below Mrs Knowles's garden, among the chestnut trees. This is being fitted with hydrant connections, for fire use, and when there are no heath-fires we can bathe in it: 40 feet by 7 by 5. I hope to roof it with glass, or leaves will choke it.

"Mrs Knowles had taken the plants from the cottage garden, and I have made several cuttings of bushes and limbs of trees. But there is too much growth for a week-end to cope with. I would like to spend two nights there, some month.

"I have decided to take a lease of the other side of the road, all the tree-grown part, for £15 a year: and Godwin is preparing the lease. My water-works made this necessary. The ram is working very well.

"Mrs Hardy and Miss Fetherstonhaugh send messages. Both are well and at home. I see them very seldom now, but found them both on one afternoon a month ago. Arnie is coming to Clouds Hill this autumn. I wrote and told him the place is too unfinished. Also he might be disturbed by there being no bed or food-preparing place. I must say I find the ruling-out of beds a great success. The little room upstairs where you used to sleep is going to become a work-room, I think, with cupboards for clothes and a food-table – bread, cheese, butter and jams: also fruit.

"I think that is all the news. I work at boats always, and am now getting my ideas generally accepted..."

By the year's close the climate of southern England had moved on from heath-fires into prolonged frost, Lawrence told his mother in a letter of 17 December 1993:

"It has lately been howling cold in England: the ice on the sea has been thick on all the beaches and mud flats. Clouds Hill spring froze over, for the first time in my experience. The water is now very feebly flowing, smaller than I have known it. It is sad, just when my bath had been put in. We dare not use it, till more rain falls. Cities like Liverpool are cutting off their water every afternoon, and hundreds of villages are carting water.

"I am just back from the cottage, which is now finished, at last, and looking untidy but well. The new zipp-bedding [leather sleeping bags] is a great success. Pat cannot finish the water-tank (to be known as Shaw's Puddle) because of the frost, which would kill the cement. It is almost finished, however, and will come to little harm, in its present state. Such a relief to have the cottage to myself, at last, after all these months of workmen and upset. If there is ever anything more to do, I shall do it myself.

"No letter from you for some weeks but no news of trouble in your part of China. I hope the 'Red' party may get the upper hand quickly and settle down into something Chinese. It is the only hope I can see, as against Japanisation. No matter, though. There is a new rather good Scotch novel out, about Ross-shire and the expulsion of the crofters. I shall probably send it to you to keep the [J. M.] Barrie and [Norman] Douglas company. Your bank I saw a few weeks ago. It says it has done just what you want, rather against its judgement. No matter, again.

"Both your cheques came. I am sorry you made them so big. The *Odyssey* is paying for Clouds Hill improvements, wholly, I hope. I shall know by the end of the month, when the last bill comes in.

"Everything to date has been paid for, as it was finished: so there should not be too much to come. You will find the little place so different: I'm afraid it will not be so suitable for you two: but it fits me like a glove: and if you do want to return to Dorset, and give me warning, I will find you somewhere near. A lovely district."

Eric Kennington recalled this period. He too had seen little of Lawrence, he told the Atlantic Monthly of April 1937, but "he was continually present spiritually, with help, understanding, joy & jokes. His physical presence – though it, like his letter, spelled happiness – seemed unnecessary."

Asking for tea-spoons

Lawrence was to see little of Dorset in 1934. On 2 February he wrote that he had not been to the cottage for a month, in another of his exceptionally detailed letters to his mother in China:

"The Air Ministry still allow me a reasonably free hand with boats and engines and so they get the boats and engines that I want, and not always what they want. I have just over a year of time to serve, and shall then fall quietly into Clouds Hill and stay quiet for a while, to see what it feels like. I have a queer sense that it is all over – all the active part of my life, I mean; and that retirement from the R.A.F. is also retirement from the stream. I shall be 46; which is neither young nor old; too young to be happy doing nothing, but too old for a fresh start.

However there is nothing that I want to do, and nothing particularly that I am glad to have done. So I am unlikely to live either in the past or in the future. Man is not an animal in which intelligence can take much pride. The cottage is finished, so long as its main lines go. The tinkering with details will be distraction for my leisure. You see, since I grew up I have never been at leisure at all. It will be a radical and not very enjoyable change.

"Sometimes I think of writing a little picture of the R.A.F. and sometimes of wandering across England and Scotland by Brough and afoot. There will be time for both things, won't there? By rearranging my investments I shall bring their yield up to £2 a week, and that will easily keep me. Thanks to the R.A.F. and its twelve years of simple company, I have learnt to be very comfortable on little. I have settled on £2 a week because that leaves me free of income tax.

"I have not seen the cottage for a month, so cannot tell if Pat [Knowles] has finished the water-pool (Shaw's Puddle we are going to call it, in derision) whose brick-work was held up by the frost. We have made it nearly forty feet long and seven feet wide, to hold 7,000 gallons.

"It lies under the chestnut trees below the wild end of Mrs Knowles' garden, just opposite my long upstairs window. For the moment its shows, rather; but there is a bank of rhododendrons in front of it, and in two years or so it will be quite invisible from the cottage and the road. It is only two feet lower than the ram, and so has a good fall all over the park.

"I have put a fire hydrant thread on the outlet pipe, so that the Tank Corps can run a hose straight out from it. And in warm weather Bill [Bray, or Bugg] will be able to swim in it – all supposing the cement does not crack and disappoint us.

"The Arab doors [brought by Lawrence from Jeddah] are going to close one end of the glass house that covers the pool. Parsons, Mrs Hardy's carpenter, is repairing them. More expense: but I hated to have them lying about, wasted."

On 5 March 1934 Lawrence wrote to Miss L. P. Black in Torquay, again from his lodgings at 13 Birmingham Street, Southampton, to thank her for a pudding. He proceeds to commission from her a set of four tea-spoons: "Now about my cottage! Please, no furniture. I have had great satisfaction and some exasperation in building everything that goes into the place. Fenders, chairs, table, couches. It has two rooms and two of everything, accordingly; the whole place is designed for just the single inhabitant! It has neither rugs nor paint nor plaster nor wallpaper. Panelling; bookshelves; bare wood and undyed leather. A queer place, but great fun. No pictures and no ornaments.

"However I agree that you ought to be associated with some item of its interior: your kindness over so many years must be perpetuated. And I went there last Thursday and sat and thought. Tea-spoons, it is: and as tea is for visitors there should be four of them, I think. As yet I have no tea-cups or plates, but I have found a pottery near Poole [Sibley Pottery, Sandford, near Wareham] and a month ago I threw a sample cup and saucer, which is drying. When it dries well, I hope to glaze it with galena [lead ore, since banned for this purpose], a lustrous brown-black which I used with great success before the war for earthenware – and then I shall have a decent tea-service.

"So if you agree, will you send me four plainish tea-spoons for four black tea-cups-to-be? It will be a very pleasant service and memory. Not yet memorial, while we are both alive and kicking; but memory, certainly."

Lawrence gave his mother a further deluge of facts about the new Clouds Hill water system in a letter from Southampton on 21 March 1934:

"England has been wet – at last. After a year of drought we have had a wettish fortnight ... not solidly wet, but with heavy rains between spells of sun and cold wind.

"I have not been to Clouds Hill lately, but it pleases me to imagine its spring running stronger. It was down to 13 gallons an hour, and weakening daily. I was fearing its total failure in the summer: and all risk is not yet past. But things are better, far better. The ram may work again. We had to stop it off, to let the spring fill.

"Pat has finished the great storage tank, and filled it from the overflow. So we have 7,000 gallons to help us through the summer. Now he is roofing it in glass. It will look ugly, from the upstairs window of the cottage, as it rises between the chestnut trees and wild end of the Knowles' garden; but in front of it is a bank of rhododendron, already five feet high, and we have planted others to make a covering wall. In three years nobody will suspect the tank.

"The Jeddah doors are to close one end of the tank, forming its north wall. They face inwards, and therefore make one side of the small glass study of mine which ends the tank-house. They will open, if their covering doors are first opened – and then they will throw the study and the tank into connection with the air and the bushes. Parsons, the carpenter, has mended the edges of the doors, and patched them with cedar, of much the same tint as the old wood. I think they will look magnificent. Pat is erecting them. The job costs money, but I am so glad to have found a use for them, after all ..."

Brother Arnold and his wife had visited Clouds Hill and used the lavatory: "I think they liked the cottage and its new fittings – but they emptied the cistern (poor Ram not working) and had to carry their water. They had their Morris Minor and went out for meals."

A further epistle about Clouds Hill, mentioning its temporary tenants, was sent to his mother from Southampton on 6 April 1934. She had been giving exceedingly close attention to the textbook technology of the fire hydrant, and puzzled how he was going to persuade water to flow uphill:

"There, it is a Saturday and late in the evening. I am at Southampton, in my lodgings, with a little fire against the cold of the night. At Clouds Hill Mrs Roberts is inhabiting the cottage. She arrived unexpectedly, after a holiday at Weymouth which exhausted her money and drove Roberts himself back to London to raise more. She moved to Winfrith to await it – and came to see Mrs Knowles on the Thursday when I was at last able to reach Clouds Hill after three weeks in the North and at sea. I suggested she move to the cottage for a few days, till the money comes. It will not be long – for on the 14th [Jock] Chambers (ex-R.A.F.) comes to the cottage for a fortnight's camping holiday.

"Two letters of yours came, almost together. By them I learn that your two years abroad may lengthen. I had been expecting you home soon, and was beginning to wonder where you would settle to live. The cottage will be my home, then; and I have arranged it accordingly, to fit me. It will be difficult even to put up a visitor, the place is so 'one-man' now. Probably when you come to see it, I shall give you the cottage, and camp myself in the little work-room by the pool.

"The cottage is nearly finished. The book-room lacks only its fender-cum-log-box. Then it is complete. The bath-room lacks only its bath-mat; and the boiler its final lagging of asbestos plaster. The upstairs room is complete, but for its beam-candle-sconce.

"The food-room alone remains to arrange. I plan to sheath its walls with aluminium foil: to fit an old ship's-bunk across the dark end, complete with drawers: to arrange its food-shelf, its table, perhaps a chair.

"Then the Clouds Hill cottage is finished – no, I forgot a cast-iron fireback for the book-room, and an air-vent to make the fire draw. But these are all small jobs, and could be finished in two months, if I had the time for them. As it is, I can attend to the place only by fits and starts, and so it drags on interminably.

"Our last doing was to sheath the bath-room walls in sheet cork, laid on in slabs twelve inches by seven, and a sixteenth of an inch thick. The cork cost about 15 shillings, and has done the job excellently. Its grain and colour are beautiful. I do not know how age will change it. Today it is as good as any room I've seen.

"We have also hung the door-leathers to the book-room and the upstairs room, on hinged door-rods of wrought iron. They are in natural cow-hide, and very successful. Pat works steadily at roofing the water-pool, which has now been full for six weeks, and does not leak at all. That is 7,000 gallons of water.

"Your letter asks how would we make it flow up-hill, if there is a fire? Why, by the camp fire-engine, which is a powerful pump. In an hour it would pump the whole pool dry – but that hour's water would probably save our places.

"The pool is not finished: it has still to be rendered over inside in fine cement; but we will not do that till the roof is finished, as rain or cold or the dust of a high wind would damage the final cementing.

"So Pat is now roofing it, slowly and single-handed. He has nearly finished the wooden framing and the sash-bars. Next week the floors of my little study at its N.end, and the entrance-porch at the S. end will be laid.

"The the Jeddah gates go in, to form the N. wall. They are just the right width, though unnecessarily high. However we cannot cut them down, so we have made the study too high, instead. Then the glass will arrive, and be fixed into place. Then the pool is finished. About May 15, I think. The last act will be to visit my Bank and find out what income I shall have left, to live on, after it all. Of course, at the worst, I can do some sort of editing or translating work, to help me out.

"Meanwhile we have the tanks running back & forward along my hill-top boundary, to tear a bare way through the heather and heath. This will make an efficient fire-guard, against fires sweeping in across the plain.

"So between this and the water-pool I shall feel safer, this year. The weather is still dry, and it bodes badly for the summer, from the point of fires.

"Already there has been a fire near Bere Regis, besides several in

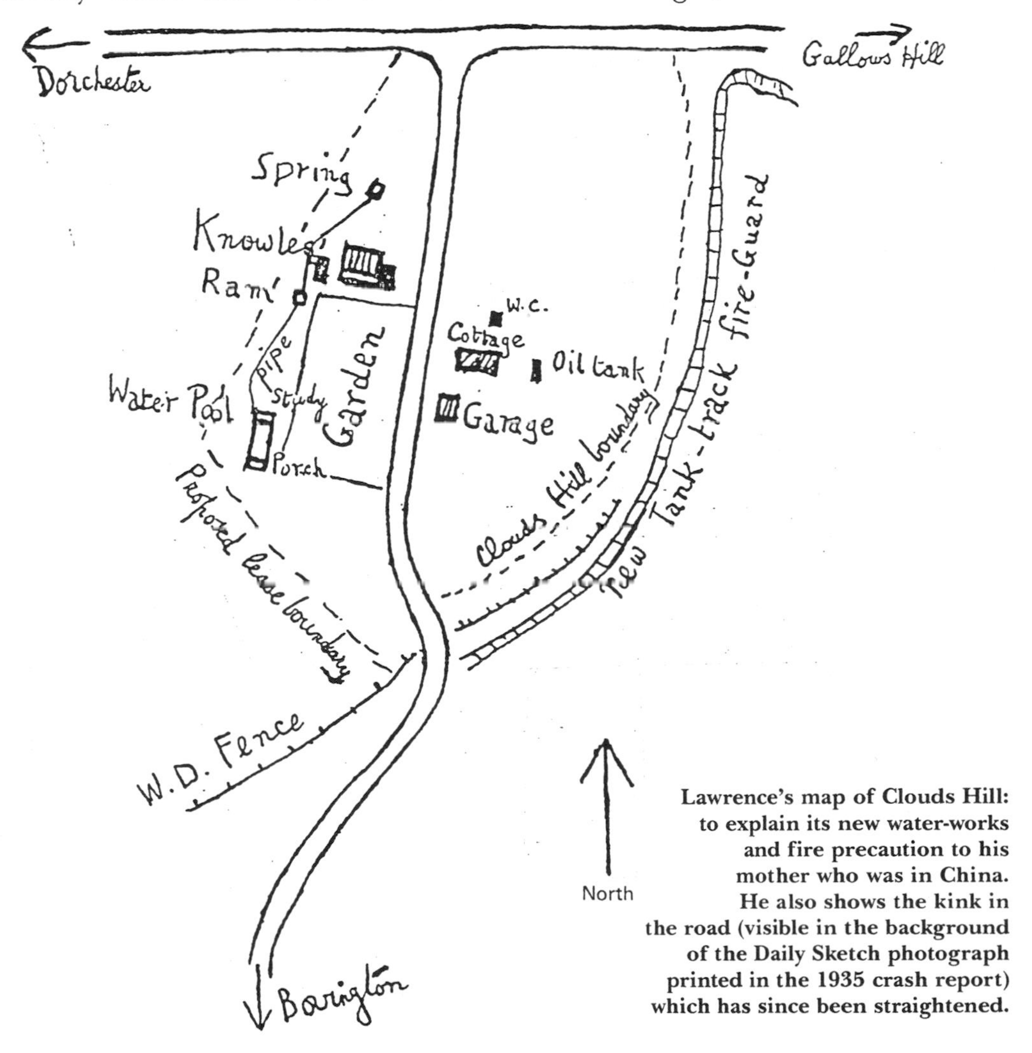

Lawrence's map of Clouds Hill: to explain its new water-works and fire precaution to his mother who was in China. He also shows the kink in the road (visible in the background of the Daily Sketch photograph printed in the 1935 crash report) which has since been straightened.

Hampshire and Kent. My spring is improving a little thanks to rains in March. It is up to about 450 gallons a day, as against 350. Normal is between seven and eight hundred.

"I fear we shall not see that this year; but I feel that a total failure of the supply is now unlikely. If we have a normal summer, with some wet spells, we should get through successfully."

As an afterthought to this note – some note – Lawrence again wrote to his mother on 17 April 1934 with a sketch-map to aid the explanation of the mighty plan of campaign that had brought water into his Dorset oasis:

"I sent you an account of the new Clouds Hill works in my last note, about a week ago. Here is a sketch-map to show you how they lie. I have marked-in a line of what land, on the W. side of the road, I want to lease from Godwin [agent for the Moreton Estate]. He agrees, and the rent of £15 per annum is agreed too: but of course that is as far as it has got.

"I send him a telegraph or two occasionally, just to keep my end up, but am not pressing him, for so soon as he does produce the lease my rent will begin – and his delay now is saving me money.

"What I have marked off is about three acres, so I am not getting it particularly cheaply – except that the land would fetch much more, if a row of bungalows was built on it."

By 1934 he was "despairing of ever using the cottage I lent for July ... and for August". Additionally, he told Florence Hardy on 27 July: "I have been in Dorset only for an occasional hour, not even my traditional weekends have been possible. My cottage is ready for March 1935 when I leave the service and fall back on it as home. I think it is pleasantly ready, full of books and tinned music, with a bath and chairs and all manner of comforts ..."

There would be weightier matters than cups and saucers, and that reservoir amid the rhododendrons that so fascinated his mother, for Lawrence to ponder over in a characteristic bout of nervous hyperactivity that came with the spring of 1934.

Lawrence on Air Defence

Lawrence's informed insider-view on the necessary shape of the overdue revitalisation of the Air Defence of the United Kingdom in the mid-1930s is set out in detail in a letter to Lionel Curtis on 19 March 1934. He was writing from the Union Jack Club in Waterloo Road, London S.E.1. It is a masterly statement from Lawrence the military mind, showing its political and strategical precision:

"The defence question is full of snags and is being ineptly handled by Lords Rothermere and Beaverbrook. I agree that the balance of expenditure on Navy, Army and R.A.F. is wrong: but I do not want R.A.F. expenditure increased. Our present squadrons could deal very summarily with France.

When Germany wings herself – ah; that will be another matter, and our signal to reinforce: for the German kites will be new and formidable, not like that sorry French junk.

"All we need now is to keep in ourselves the capacity to expand the R.A.F. usefully. when the times make it necessary. For this we must have:

(1) Aerodromes enough, sited in the useful places.
(2) Aircraft firms well equipped, with up-to-date designers, designs and plant.
(3) Brains enough inside our brass hats to employ 1 and 2.

(1) Easy – but means another 15 aerodromes, each costing £20,000: they take about three years to bring into being.
(2) In hand; excellent; but hampered by
(3) The direction of R.A.F. and Air Ministry. Our air-marshals are rather wooden-headed, and some of the civilian A.I.D. [Air Inspection Directorate] inspectors and technicians who handle design are hopeless. Consequently our military aircraft are like Christmas trees all hung with protruding gadgets, our flying boats are a bad joke, our civil aircraft are (almost) the world's slowest; and air tactics and strategy are infantile.

"More money should be spent at once on (1) above: and research made into flying boat development (after sacking the present authorities) and wireless-controlled aircraft. Also to develop the art of sound-ranging, and anti-aircraft gunnery. If I had my way, I would constitute a new Flying Boat department of Air Ministry, and have in a dozen good naval men to give it a start.

"Upon the Navy I have views also. Our air bombs are not going to sink capital ships; but will render them useless as fighting platforms, and probably uninhabitable. This in only three or four years time. The defence of surface craft against aircraft will be found in manoeuvre – in being able to turn quicker on the water than the plane can in the air – not difficult, with small ships, as water gives you a firmer rudder. So I expect to see the surface ships of navies in the future limited to small, high-speed, manoeuvrable mosquito craft, none larger than the destroyers of today [then only around 1,250 tons].

"There are controversial points in the above, and to argue them one must consider smoke-screens, the one-pounder pom-pom, trajectories, dive-arcs, [*omission of an Official Secret, which I think may be an early reference to the detection of aircraft by reflected radio signals*]; all sorts of technical things. But I am prepared to maintain my thesis in most company. Do not, however, take this exposition of it as exhaustive or even fair. To deal with imponderables, layer on layer of imponderables, more resembles faith than arguments."

Lawrence – by instinct, temperament and intellect – inhabited a world away from the left-wing mass movement of the times, the Peace Pledge Union, which in its national ballot over the next twelve months would poll nearly half the adult population of Great Britain. In it over that period, the votes would pile up not only for disarmament but for the abolition of naval and military aircraft (Yes – 7,565,212 / No – 1,356,316) and even more overwhelmingly for the abolition of the private manufacture of arms (Yes – 8,289,455 / No – 619,653).

'I become a private citizen'

In November 1934, Lawrence wrote to Tom Beaumont of Broad Street, Dewsbury, a machine-gunner in the armoured car squadron under his command in Palestine: "On March 12, 1935, I become a private citizen, and shall have the honour and difficulty of paying for myself. My savings are on the short side, but if there is anything left for travelling expenses you will see me in Dewsbury."

Over the Christmas leave of 1934, Lawrence discussed with his friend and neighbour, Pat Knowles, the practicalities of setting up a private printing press at Clouds Hill. It would need its own shed, as there was no space in the cramped cottage, but other ideas then seemed to take his attention and he did not proceed with the matter. He was forty-six and publicly preparing for retirement; but the press was sure that there was more to it than that.

Ideas were indeed still flowing. He met the young Bradford engineer Edward Spurr and told him of the sea-skimming aerodynamic boat that he visualised speeding over the water on a cushion of air. Spurr was working on the same concept, which would come into being as the hovercraft, and when the makers R. Malcolm Limited of Slough launched their futuristic "Empire Day" speed-boat on 24 May 1938 she had an inscription on her nose: "To L. of A. – à compte."

'Damn the Press'

On 13 February 1935, Lawrence let slip to his friend Aircraftman W. Bradbury that he was in contact with the intelligence department at the Air Ministry. "Air Ministry warns me that the Press are getting curious about my movements again," Lawrence wrote. "Damn the Press." It was, as Winston Churchill observed, this knack he had for "backing into the limelight".

In the first week of March 1935, ex-Aircraftman 338171 Shaw, Lawrence of Arabia – "one of the greatest mystery men of the age," as the press continued to remind the public – left R.A.F. Bridlington, North Humberside, on his bicycle. He had been working for four months at the

Lawrence on his bike:
pushing off from R.A.F. Bridlington
into 'retirement' appealed to the media.
This photograph was taken by his friend Ian Deheer.

harbourside on the target-towing boats that were used for the offshire bombing range.

Lawrence was on his push-bike, he told Basil Liddell Hart, because "without his service pay he would have to give up the luxury of running a high-powered motor cycle". That resolve was short-lived; it was merely for press and public consumption. Lawrence knew how to manipulate the media when it suited him. "I never once saw him on a push-cycle," Bill Bugg of Bovington told me in 1968.

En route between Humberside and Clouds Hill, he was staying in London S.E.1, when on 6 March 1935 he wrote to Florence Hardy:

"I should like to call, but cannot. The press-people are snooping round Clouds Hill, taking its picture and looking for me, to take mine. So I will have to keep up in London and the Midlands for the next few weeks. As soon as I safely can I want to settle down in the little cottage for a long spell, and try to find out what there is left for me now the R.A.F. is ended.

"Meanwhile I'm feeling lost – like an evicted hermit-crab! If you want to send the *Indiscretion* [Hardy's first novel, *The Poor Man and the Lady*, then being published but under a different title], will you please post it to Clouds Hill, marked 'to await return'. My shiftings about will be many and abrupt, probably: and I do not want it exposed to the risk of missing me. Sooner or later (and I hope sooner ... pressmen have little staying power) I'll be able to get home.

"Yes, poor Mrs Knowles [deceased Clouds Hill neighbour] is a loss. She was very much a friend. Her eldest son, Pat, hopes to acquire a 'Mrs Knowles' of his own shortly [Joyce], and if so they will settle in the family bungalow and continue its tradition. I hope so. If they do, I'll help them rebuild it into shapeliness and permanency – as permanency in building goes!"

Lawrence was embarking upon an active retirement. "My shiftings will be many and abrupt," contrasts with the public side of the man who left Bridlington on a push-bike. The press might be to blame for his avoidance of going to Max Gate, but more likely they were the convenient excuse.

Lawrence also wrote to Ernest Thurtle on 6 March 1935, this time expressing sadness at having left the Royal Air Force: "My Dorset 'fastness' is beset, they tell me by the pressmen: so I wander about London in a queer unrest, wondering if my mainspring will ever have a tension in it again.

"So I'm not cheerful actually; but sad at losing my R.A.F. existence. It was good, and I felt useful: also it was noticeably peaceful. I expect there is a good deal to be said for the comfortable shadow of a 'bombing place' – now a term of abuse, but the only democratic weapon!

"Thank you for the book. I look forward to reading it when I get home ... which is after the ink-slingers go to their homes. Theodore Powys [who had just published *Captain Patch*], the brother of Llewelyn, is a rare person."

Lawrence was desperate to be left alone – or rather to be allowed to

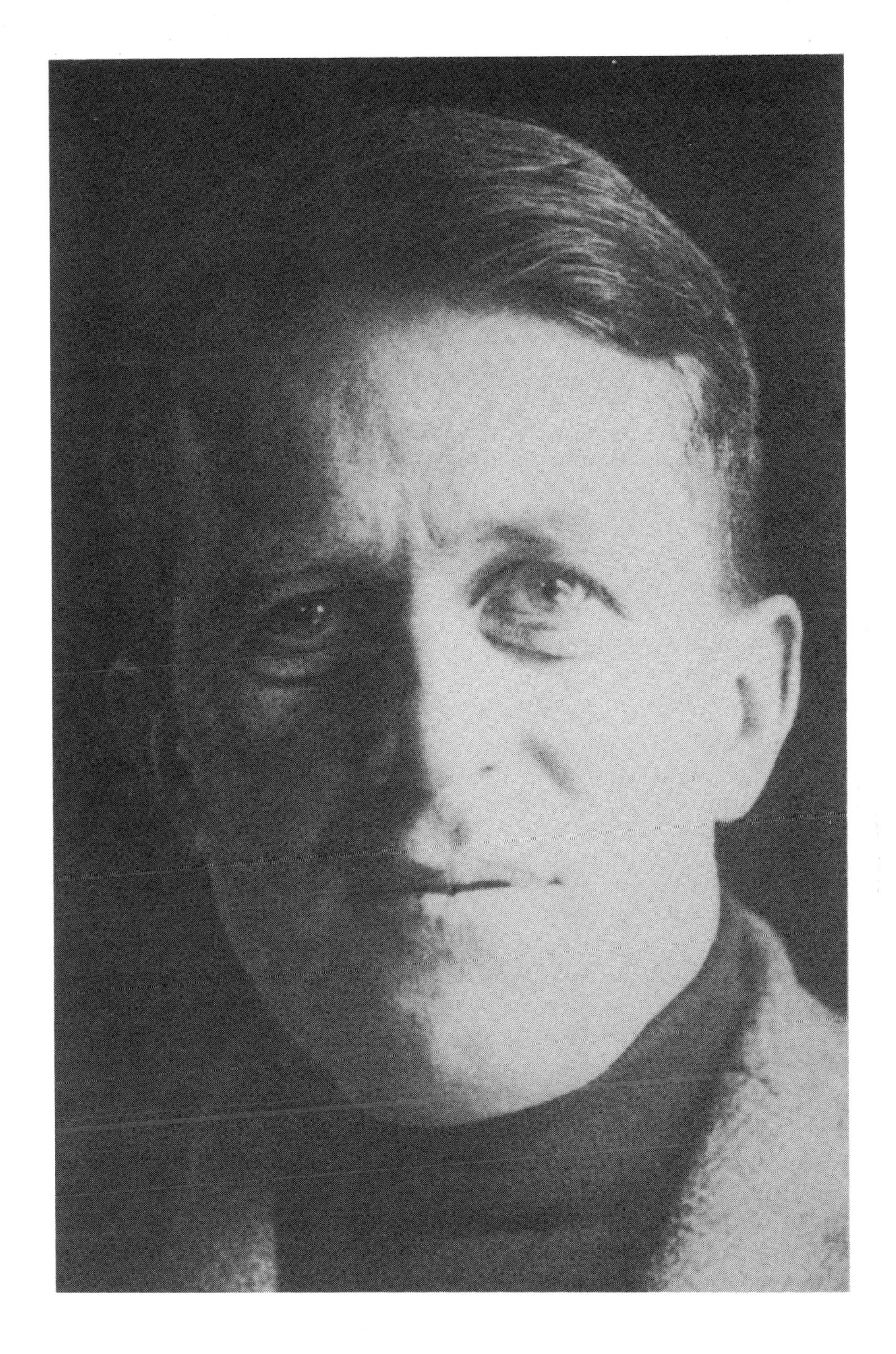

Lawrence in February 1935: from his last set of portraits, apparently taken by Flight-Lieutenant Reginald Sims at his cottage in Hornsea, Yorkshire.

continue with his life unobserved. Had it been merely to protect a retirement he could have ignored them but for some reason he went on the offensive and visited London 19 March 1935 to plead with the newshounds for some privacy:

"I've spent all day today with the Press Association bosses, and Press Photographing Agencies, making quite a lot of ground. There are good hopes, I fancy, of persuading all of them to leave me alone, and to refuse to buy the stolen products of the free-lancers."

When he returned to Clouds Hill he found the situation unchanged and wrote to Esmond Harmsworth, the chairman of the press barons' club, the Newspaper Proprietors' Association:

"Unfortunately, the quietude has been a complete failure. Reporters and press photographers have visited the place in some numbers, anxious to photograph it and me, or to ascertain my future intentions. This is a very simple district and their enquiries after me have given my country neighbours only too much to talk about. Their eagerness to find me drove me out; and after I had gone it led them to break the tiles of my roof, split the door and trample all over my patch of land in search of me. I have had to ask the local police to patrol the place, in my absence. I am writing to ask if your association can help to relieve me of some of this attention?

"I quite realise that many of the visitors are freelances: but even these find their market in the biggest newspapers. It would be a great comfort to me if editors could generally deny me further space."

Lawrence summed up the situation in a letter to John Buchan on 1 April 1935:

"My life? Not too good. The Press were besetting this cottage when I reached it. I went to London for a while: they desisted. I returned: they did. The most exigent of them I banged in the eye, and while he sought a doctor I went off again on my wanderings, seeing the Newspaper Society, and the Photographic Agencies, and Esmond Harmsworth (for the Newspaper Proprietors' Assn.) with the plea to leave me alone. They agree, more or less, so long as I do nothing that earns a new paragraph: and on that unholy compact I am back here again in precarious peace, and liking a life that has no fixed point, no duty and no time to keep."

Just before he died in early 1981, Pat Knowles recalled that counter-attack for Michael Yardley. "Come on Pat, let's be rid of them," said Lawrence. There were two reporters outside. Following the fight, Lawrence was white and trembling. His anger had been replaced by shock and he held his head in his hands. "Pat," he said, "It's years since I hit a man."

6 May 1935 was King George V's silver jubilee and Lawrence wrote to Eric Kennington that night: "All over bonfires, the beautiful Dorset, to-night. Twenty-six, I think, so far, from my window. Ah well, poor George!

"Don't bother about those drawings. Leave it a little while till I revive my humanities and come up and see you. I plan a raid on Holly Copse, to stay with you for a night or two ... possible? At your discretion, absolutely: but I do not want to interfere with your development as a nurse. What is the illness? I do hope (by your light-hearted reference to it) that it's either over or safe.

"The tympanum sounds good. I wonder what it is in. Stone goes out of date slowly, I think.

"You wonder what I am doing? Well, so do I, in truth. Days seem to dawn, suns to shine, evenings to follow, and then I sleep. What I have done, what I am doing, what I am going to do, puzzle me and bewilder me. Have you ever been a leaf and fallen from your tree in autumn and been really puzzled by it? That's the feeling.

"The cottage is all right for me ... but how on earth I'll ever be able to put anyone up baffles me. There cannot ever be a bed, a cooking vessel, or a drain in it – and I ask you ... are not such things essential to life ... necessities? Peace to everybody."

I have quoted this letter in full because of its penultimate paragraph, containing the reference to the leaf falling from the tree in autumn, which is both prophetic and if taken out of context could almost be interpreted as a suicide note. I see it, however, as a typical Lawrence letter, saying very little very nicely and leaving his options open should he need a bed for the night, whilst making sure that his friend will not expect reciprocal treatment at Clouds Hill.

It was Eric Kennington who most acutely sensed Lawrence's aversion to ageing. "Who's that poor old chap," he had asked of a vigorous 60-year-old. "Old age to him was pathetic," Kennington would write in *T. E. Lawrence by his Friends*. "T.E. hoped not to live to grow old. That meant anything over 45."

Hiding in the Clouds Hill bushes in the second week of May 1935 was one Peter Page, but I think he was more than a reporter.

Peter Page: spying on Clouds Hill for MI5?

In 1968 the mystery of Peter Page's clothes, found in a dustbin hidden in the heath at Clouds Hill on Saturday 11 May 1935, two days before Lawrence's crash, emerged in print in the second issue of Dorset County Magazine. I cannot recall quite how the information reached the magazine office, which was then my parents' bungalow at Headswell Crescent in Bournemouth, because we were not the original recipients of the letter we printed. It was on newspaper copy-paper from "John Prentice c/o Evening News office, Portsmouth. 15/1/68." The letter must have been passed to us by the Hampshire County Magazine in Southampton. It starts, "My dear Dennis"; the magazine's editor was Dennis Stevens. I will print it in full:

"I hope you remember a handsome young man who looked after the

Fareham Branch of the News for eighteen years. Even if you do not, John Prentice remembers you and your landlady near Capt. Vian's house in the Botley area.

"Well, I have just made contact with an old friend who left for Jamaica in '36, and I went to India. The year before that we were associated with what I have always thought was a real mystery and although it occurred in Bovington (Dorset) it might be useful for your magazine. Here goes –

"In 1935, my friend Duncan Montagu Cake and I were serving with the R.A.O.C. and undergoing a Tank Recovery Course at Clouds Hill, near Wool, in Dorset. My Sealyham bitch, Gin, was in camp with me, and she was connected with the incident. It was a beautiful sunny afternoon, a Saturday, when we were off duty, and being country lovers it was decided to 'cut across the bracken and swamps' to Moreton, just to see the house where Lawrence of Arabia had his home.

"Suitably dressed, we had gone a mile or so, when Gin sniffed out an object partially covered by bracken. Closer inspection revealed a dustbin, the large type used by occupants of military married quarters. It could only have been manually carried over the swamp as the road, lined with rhododendrons leading to Moreton, was a long way away. In the far distance Monty and I saw only a lady with a dog – nothing or nobody else.

"I removed the dustbin lid, and took out a parcel, neatly tied with string which I untied, throwing the string some distance away in the undergrowth.

"By this time, my friend was doing something similar with a second parcel in the bin. Mine contained a neatly folded civilian suit, shirt and socks. His had other items of male underwear and a trilby hat, also pressed. There was no footwear. Inside the hat was clearly inked the name 'Peter Page'.

"Bearing in mind that in those days there were some 'queer people' about, we allowed Gin to have a sniff, then replaced the wrapping minus the string, carrying on to our rendezvous – Moreton House. We made our way back by a different route, arriving at Clouds Hill, as our officers were at dinner in their Marquee Mess. We contacted Mr Beahan who was orderly officer.

"The day was still bright and warm, and Mr Beahan suggested we go back to the dustbin – if it were still there – then he would report our discovery to the local policeman. We went back, and imagine our surprise when there was no dustbin, and also no string! Somewhere, hidden, the mysterious dustbin owner had been watching us.

"We told Lieutenant Beahan, and as far as he was concerned the incident was closed. But not as far as Monty Cake and I were concerned! On the Sunday morning we reported to the local Military Police, and after their extensive enquiries we were told by them that 'No Peter Page was known locally'.

"Although nearly 33 years have passed, the memory and the details are vivid, and I often wonder 'Who was Peter Page?' and what the ... was he up to! John Prentice, 9 Westfield Avenue, Fareham."

It is more than a coincidence that Peter Page was one of the best sleuths in Grub Street. Arnold Bennett had recommended him to Lord Beaverbrook on 24 October 1923:

"There is a fellow named Peter Page on the Daily Sketch that I think would be better employed on the Standard [one of Beaverbrook's papers]. I don't know him personally. He has a considerable subterranean reputation in Fleet Street." Such abilities, and the cover a journalist's trade provides for being anywhere in the land, must equally have drawn him to the attention of the recruiting sergeants for MI5.

I am sure we have found our Peter Page, and half sure that he was more than a newspaperman.

Lawrence: Director Designate of proposed Intelligence Directorate

The watcher of Clouds Hill, Peter Page, would have needed his other set of clothes – the rugged outdoor sort he was wearing – for espionage in the damp and prickly Clouds Hill slope. There is so much rhododendron around the tiny cottage that it must have been quite a simple task to slip in from only a few feet away when the occupant had made his noisy exit, to find and read recent correspondence. Likewise the rider's noisy return would have been loud enough to give adequate warning for slipping back into the bushes.

Which of course begs a question. Why on earth should MI5 be watching a 46-year-old odd-ball hero who only two months before, on 12 March 1935, had told the world he was in retirement?

Lawrence used the press to sow contradictions that reduced his life to a public soap opera; whenever he had the chance of dropping a lie he would habitually take it up, and then immediately move on to the next. This both amused and protected him. No one was taking T. E. Lawrence seriously, except that is Peter Page and his colleagues.

MI5 knew, as the press only suspected in its wildest flights of fancy, that Colonel Thomas Edward Lawrence was being groomed for the nation's top secret job. He was Director Designate of the proposed Intelligence Directorate which was being shaped to put espionage services on a war footing and co-ordinate the general monitoring of German penetration in Britain.

In those shadows the real T. E. Lawrence was able to slip into a more serious game. He was once more his nation's servant.

Colonel Richard Meinertzhagen's *Middle East Diary*, a highly sensitive and secret document which he entrusted to the care of Rhodes House Library in Oxford, confirms that in May 1935 T. E. Lawrence was at the head of a review panel considering the entire restructuring of the British secret intelligence services:

"We worked together in the C.O. [Colonial Office] on a scheme for a Directorship of Intelligence embracing both political and military aspects and coalescing under one head, F.O. [Foreign Office], W.O. [War Office], Admiralty, Air Ministry, Scotland Yard and MI5. Put the thing to Churchill, Amery, Macdonogh, they concurred. Involved training college in London and one in the country. It was complete and we were applying for Treasury sanction when T.E. died. I felt I could not go on with it as it was very much his work."

Meinertzhagen's statement elevates Lawrence out of innocent retirement and restores him at the centre of this country's most secret preparations of its contingency plans for the anticipated war with Germany.

It makes a nonsense of at least the first half of Lawrence's brother Arnold's denial which was printed by the Daily Sketch on 20 May 1935: "Mr A. W. Lawrence yesterday denied that Lawrence was engaged in Secret Service work or had recently visited Berlin."

'England's master spy'

The Germans had no such reticence. There the newspapers were referring to Lawrence as "England's master spy". Indeed the silence of the news blackout surrounding the six days Lawrence lay dying in Bovington military hospital led to speculation that he had been spirited out of the country and was in fact preparing for surreptitious British intervention in the gathering storm in the Horn of Africa. Italian troops would invade Abyssinia on 3 October; France was already negotiating to cede part of its French Somaliland colony to Italy, along with shares in the Ethiopian Railway.

Not that Lawrence's death would be sufficient to stop the speculation. Sir Reader Buller, the British Consul in Marrakesh, reported in his autobiography, *The Camels Must Go,* "a tale from an Italian fascist rag published in Marrakesh, to the effect that T. E. Lawrence was not dead, but under cover of a faked funeral had been smuggled out of England and sent to Ethiopia to stir up trouble against Italy."

Edward Robinson, in *Lawrence the Rebel,* notes that he was to be spirited yet further across the world, as another newspaper reported: "The man in hospital was not Lawrence, who is on a secret mission in the Far East."

A dangerous political indiscretion

There was also the German problem, over which Lawrence had been pondering that fateful weekend of 11 May 1935.

He spent the weekend at Clouds Hill and apparently had no guests. Later in the month, on Saturday 25 May, he had been invited by Lady Astor to Cliveden, beside the Thames, to discuss the upheaval planned "to reorganise the Defence Forces", but seems to have had no wish to be lobbied by her and certainly from the character of the man as we know it he would recoil from the thought of a weekend of high living with the Cliveden set plus Prime Minister Stanley Baldwin. "No," he wrote to Nancy Astor on 8 May 1935, "wild mares would not at present take me away from Clouds Hill ... Also there is something broken in the works, as I told you: my will, I think. In this mood I would not take on any job at all, so do not commit yourself to advocating me, lest I prove a non-starter."

A word-artist of the calibre of T. E. Lawrence does not accidentally infer that Lady Asor is a "wild mare". It is a letter from Lawrence distancing himself, in self-protection, by maintaining his public posture. He had nothing to gain from providing Cliveden gossip, particularly if he was already involved, as Richard Meinertzhagen would state, in a re-structuring of the entire British secret security services.

On Sunday 12 May 1935 Lawrence wrote from Clouds Hill to Sir Karl Parker at the Ashmolean Museum, Oxford: "At present, I'm sitting in my cottage and getting used to an empty life."

Lawrence was, for once, being consistent. Or at least as far as was necessary to fend off the constant claims on his company. Yet there was still the highly-mobile T. E. Lawrence. He had some reason for riding up to Catterick Camp in Yorkshire, or at least that is what he told the Bovington butcher, F .J. Stratton, on Monday 13 May 1935. I think he was intending to ride up there that afternoon but postponed the idea in order to see Henry Williamson as soon as possible, in fact the very next day.

In a 1968 letter to Colin Graham, Mr Stratton says that on the morning of the fatal accident Lawrence told him he would be spending the afternoon on the road to Catterick. That would be after he had eaten the two chops he had just bought for lunch. The feat would demand an average speed of 80 miles per hour if he were to be there by 5 pm. I think Lawrence mentioned Catterick because he was in the process of thinking himself out of the journey. For he had just sent a telegram from the post office at Bovington Camp to the novelist Henry Williamson, who lived near Barnstaple, inviting him to Clouds Hill the next day, Tuesday 14 May 1935: "11.25 AM 13 MAY 1935. WILLIAMSON SHALLOWFORD FILLEIGH. LUNCH TUESDAY WET FINE COTTAGE ONE MILE NORTH BOVINGTON CAMP. SHAW."

Williamson, who was born in 1897 and had served in the Flanders trenches, had won the Hawthornden Prize in 1928 with *Tarka the Otter*. Politically he held extreme right wing views and would become a close friend of Sir Oswald Mosley, whose British Union of Fascists he had supported from the first, and would follow to the end. He had written to Lawrence asking him to come to Germany to meet Hitler, to "Send him along the proper track."

'Hitler meeting' letter vanishes

That crucial letter is missing, Williamson told a journalist from The Times who met him in May 1968, on one of his rare old-age visits to London from his Ox's Cross home at Georgeham in North Devon. The paper reported: "Williamson's letter to Lawrence was never recovered from Lawrence's effects: it disappeared, and to this day Williamson has no idea what happened to it."

The fascist Henry Williamson was a dangerous contact for Britain's leading national hero. The slide towards anti-semitism had gripped the British Union of Fascists. Violence had marred its great Olympia rally and the split between Sir Oswald Mosley and Lord Rothermere had cost the movement its major press platforms.

By its support for the Röhm purge the British Union of Fascists was now firmly identified with the Nazis and therefore with Hitler. At a stroke Mosley had thrown away his patriotic card. In the Albert Hall in March 1935 he predicted that Britain would be Europe's next fascist state and addressed himself to the "Jewish problem" with deportation threats against those who were regarded as subverting British interests.

They were now on the slope toward the Public Order Act of 1936 and, with the war, Defence Regulation 18b under which Mosley would find himself at Brixton with unrepentant loyal henchmen such as Williamson and some notable members of the landed classes, including Dorset's Captain George Pitt-Rivers.

The reason that MI5 would in May 1935 have been interested in the Williamson–Lawrence connection was that there had been a sea-change in informed British attitudes to European politics. The previous year the London Evening News had run a competition in which readers were asked to explain "Why I like the Blackshirts" with the 250 best answers being rewarded with free tickets to Mosley's rally in the Albert Hall.

That, a year on, was an inconceivable as a national newspaper promotion as it would be today. Williamson and his ideas were beyond the pale to those who controlled Britain's secret society. MI5 was, and is, responsible for security and counter-espionage inside the United Kingdom. It would have been within its brief to be watching Lawrence. Williamson was an inappropriate intellectual bedmate for the man who was earmarked to head a reorganisation of Britain's security services into a proposed composite entity.

Williamson would feel he had caused the accident, though Lawrence's ride into Bovington was probably as much to collect his mail as to send the ill-fated telegram. In *Goodbye West Country* Williamson reflected: "And if I'd turned up at Clouds Hill in early May last year without writing to ask if he'd be at home, he might still be alive. For he left his job of masonry to send me a telegram, and crashed on the way back ..." Williamson had stood in his garage looking along the sleek black lines of his six-cylinder Alvis car and pondered. He was half inclined to drive to Dorset immediately but in the event the letter was sent. It contained a proviso, unless the day was rainy, and that was why Lawrence responded with his "wet fine" wording – after all Williamson had just told Lawrence that he was the only man in England who could keep the peace in Europe, and wars don't wait for the weather.

The crash, and the disputed 'black car'

Lawrence had his crash on the return journey to Clouds Hill from Bovington Camp at about 11.30 a.m. on Monday 13 May 1935. He had ridden his Brough Superior GW 2275 three-quarters of a mile north from the end of the camp, that is from the point where the building line abruptly ends in 1997 as it did in 1935. The crash site was on open heathland in the parish of Turners Puddle, a hundred yards north-east from the rounded south-eastern corner of Moreton Plantation. The roadside vegetation was heather with a little gorse and a few slender young pines self-sown from the conifer plantation.

The spot is 400 yards south-south-east from Lawrence's cottage at Clouds Hill. It is 218 feet above sea level. In 1935 there was a concrete water-tank on the west side of the road just south of the crash point and Crown Hill Camp, a tented summer camp for soldiers, on the open ground on the opposite eastern side of the road.

At the end of the twentieth century there are many more plantings of dense conifers. The water tank is gone. The spot, however, is easy to find as it coincides with a break in the trees where tanks cross the road. A public footpath also crosses the road, immediately to the south of the crash spot, and is shown on the current generation of the Ordnance Survey maps, at grid reference SY 826 905. There are vestiges of the former flora, though this is less open now as gorse-scrub tends to predominate.

Beware, however, of misinformation. Whatever and whosoever may say it, the tendency over the years to shift the crash point 200 yards closer to the cottage is erroneous; the 400 yards is the figure recorded by the police at the time and tallies with contemporary photographs and the location of the temporary Crown Hill Camp.

The second piece of common misinformation is that the road has changed course at this point. This is utter rubbish. It is wider but is as straight now as it was then, and indeed followed the course that is shown by the six inches to the mile Ordnance Survey map of Victorian times. Straightening did take place, not at the actual 400 yards crash point but at the phoney alternative one only 150 yards from the cottage. There, in the dip, it used to kink into a bend on the east side of the present road as it drew level with the Moreton Plantation fence where this crossed the road at the south edge of the Clouds

Crown Hill Camp: the tented summertime camping ground on the east side of the road between Bovington Camp and Clouds Hill – from which Corporal Ernest Catchpole would witness Lawrence's inexplicable crash. The picture is from 'Bovington Tanks' by George and Anne Forty.

Hill plot.

This road to Clouds Hill was known as Tank Park Road, because during the Twenties the heathland on the east side had been a graveyard for machines brought back from the Western Front, which had taken years for a team of breakers to work their way through.

The section of road that became Lawrence's crash site was and is perfectly straight. It rises out of Bovington Camp in a long northerly incline. The initial crash spot, the point where the collision took place between Lawrence's motor-cycle and the rear wheel of a boy bicyclist who was travelling in the same northerly direction towards Clouds Hill, is on the Bovington side of the brow of the incline. It is marked close by, on the east side of a now greatly widened carriageway, by a commemorative oak planted by Tom Beaumont on 13 May 1983 next to a tiny roadside car-park. In the roadway at this point any cyclists would have been clearly visible for half a mile to anyone approaching from the south, from Bovington Camp.

The kinetic energy of that crash meant that the site of body impact with the tarmac, and the point where Lawrence would be picked up beside a tree, were bound to be on the Clouds Hill side of the collision spot. This final point was 50 yards further to the north immediately on the Clouds Hill side of the brow of the hill, and is shown (looking towards Clouds Hill) in the Daily Sketch photograph opposite. That sets the scene: now to describe the events.

On the road as well, in front of Lawrence and also going in a northerly direction, towards Clouds Hill, were two boys from Bovington Camp, Albert Hargraves and Frank Fletcher, on their bicycles. Frank was on his new bicycle and would move into the lead; he was accompanying his friend Albert who had been lucky enough to get a job as a butcher's boy at Bovington and was on a delivery errand. Both were aged fourteen and had

Frank Fletcher, aged 14, who was cycling with Albert Hargreaves when Lawrence of Arabia came along on a motor-cycle. Both cyclists fell. Hargreaves was injured.

Daily Sketch photographs: of the crash-site (left hand side of the road, seen looking north towards Clouds Hill where the kink has since been straightened) and bicyclist Frank Fletcher.

recently left school. Albert's father was a private at Bovington Camp and Frank lived in Moreton village. They realised a motor-cycle was approaching from the rear.

That half mile [880 yards] gentle incline up to Crown Hill Camp would have taken Lawrence thirty seconds at 60 m.p.h. During those same thirty seconds, slowly drifting along, the two bicyclists would have moved 88 yards at a speed of 6 m.p.h. or 58 yards at a 4 m.p.h. walking pace. They moved from double into single file at about 80 yards on hearing the motor-cycle.

Frank alone would be able to remember what happened as they approached Clouds Hill. His account appeared in the Dorset Daily Echo of 16 May 1935:

"We were riding in single file. I was leading. I heard a motor-cycle coming from behind and then I heard a crash. Bertie's cycle hit mine and I fell off.

"When I looked up I saw Bertie lying in the road. The motor-cycle had skidded on the other side, and the man who had gone over the handle bars had landed with his feet about five yards in from the motor-cycle which was about five yards ahead of where I fell. I got up and went to Bertie to see if he was all right. He gave me his butcher's book. I found three pence on the road. I asked Bertie if that was his money but he never answered. He seemed to go to sleep.

"I waited a minute or two, being afraid to go to the man, because his face was covered with blood. Then a man came up on a cycle and asked me to get the ambulance. But before I could go some soldiers came and he went to get it himself. A lorry came up. The men got two stretchers from some camp at the roadside and the injured man and Bertie were put on them and taken into the lorry."

The cyclist who went to Bovington Camp to fetch the ambulance does not seem to have been identified. Though he was the first to arrive at the scene of the accident, and was in all probability a local person, he would not be asked to attend the coroner's inquest. As the story unfolded it would contain "a black car" and the evidence of an independent road user might have been significant.

The following day, the Echo stated, Fletcher's father was told to prevent his son talking to the press: "The day after the accident military and civil police called on the father and told him that on no account was the boy to be interviewed by anyone without authority." Frank Fletcher described those moments again, in the 1960s, for Wareham historian Harry Broughton: "I was in front and Bert was about three yards behind me when we heard this motor-cycle coming. Bert said to keep well in for the road was not too wide and the next thing I knew Hargraves's bike hit my back wheel. As I was falling off I saw Lawrence go over the handle bars of his bike and land in a sitting position against a tree, at the same time I saw my mate lying in the middle of the road not moving at all.

"I did not know what to do first, it all happened so quickly. When I got over the shock I went over to Lawrence first. His face was covered with blood – it seemed to be coming out of his nose, but most of it was coming from the top of his head. I thought he was dead. I went over to Bert, but he was out as well. Then before I knew it there were soldiers around us. They must have come up from the tents on the far side of the road."

A hundred yards from the road, on the east side, one of those soldiers saw the motor-cycle before and immediately after the crash. Ernest Catchpole, a corporal with the Royal Army Ordnance Corps, was the only independent eye-witness who would give evidence at the inquest:

"I saw the motor-cycle which was going between 50 and 60 miles an hour. Just before the motor-cycle got level with the camp it passed a black car.

"The car, which was a private one, was going in the opposite direction and the motor-cycle got past it all right. Then I saw the motor-cycle swerve across the road to avoid two pedal-cyclists coming from Bovington. It swerved immediately after it had passed the car.

"The next thing I heard was a crash. I saw the [motor] bike twisting and turning over and over along the road. I saw nothing of the driver. I cannot swear that the driver was then on the motor-cycle.

"I ran to the scene and found the motor-cyclist on the road. His face was covered with blood which I tried to wipe away with my handkerchief.

"I sent to the camp for a stretcher, then an Army Service Corps lorry came along. I asked the driver to take the motor-cyclist to hospital. One of the pedal-cyclists was lying some distance down the road."

The two boys denied seeing any car, or, in the words of Hargraves, "any traffic of any sort". That was, is and will be, unless anyone ever admits to suppressing part of the story, the final enigma and mystery with which Thomas Edward Lawrence went to the grave. I shall take up that aspect later, and give the intriguing sequel of Corporal Catchpole's end.

Given that we have moved into an era of almost complete dominance of information dissemination by television and videos it is unfortunate that David Lean's superb film *Lawrence of Arabia* – which in 1962 revived and gently reshaped the Lawrence legend for subsequent generations – begins with a complete distortion of the location and the truth in its opening scene with Peter O'Toole on a motor-cycle. That is all it is – Peter O'Toole on a motor-cycle. Any other connection with Lawrence's fatal crash is purely coincidental. It is disappointing that Lean should be so careless with something that could easily have been handled just as dramatically with complete accuracy.

On the sixth day: 'It's all over now'

The unconscious bodies of Albert Hargraves and T. E. Lawrence were lifted on to a lorry and driven to the Military Hospital at Bovington Camp. Young Hargraves recovered consciousness and was not critically injured, though he was kept six weeks in hospital according to his employer. On the other hand he was fit enough to be released to attend the inquest on 21 May and to walk outside the courtroom to discuss comparative distances. What is certain is that his parents, though they were an army family, were kept agonising from the Monday lunchtime until the set visiting hour on Wednesday 15 May before they were allowed to visit Albert. They were not allowed to see him again until after Lawrence was dead.

X-ray photographs had been taken of Lawrence's head on the day of admission and showed a major fracture.

Lawrence's body was turned and tilted hourly by the nurses in an attempt to drain away saliva and some of the phlegm that congested one of his lungs. The crisis came on the night of Saturday 18 May. Three of the country's leading surgeons had dashed to the hospital. They were the eminent neurologist Sir Edward Farquhar Buzzard, who was the Physician in Ordinary to the King, the brain surgeon H. W. B. Cairns, and lung specialist Dr Hope Gosse.

Oxygen kept Lawrence breathing. The specialist, Captain Charles Allen, of the Royal Army Medical Corps, who had handled the case from the start, continued to maintain a bedside vigil. All knew their efforts were hopeless; the damage to his brain was irreparable. Even if he could have been kept alive he would have lost at least some of his sight and speech.

Captain Allen entered the hospital's tiny waiting room at 8.25 a.m. on Sunday 19 May and told Lawrence's friends: "It is all over now."

Wet or fine, it still meant nothing to him. The rain fell gently on to the Union Jack that wrapped his body as it was carried to a slate-roofed mortuary hut. There he was placed before an altar, beneath a small crucifix.

News of his death was sent to the King and Queen. Lawrence's 73-year-old mother still did not even know about the crash. She was steaming with her eldest son, Bob, down the Yangtze River in China. The cable containing the shock awaited their arrival in Shanghai.

The inquest: 'Accidental death'

"County of Dorset – Eastern District.
Inquest No 160.
Dated 21st May 1935.
DEPOSITIONS taken at the Inquest on view of the body of Thomas Edward Shaw of Clouds Hill, Tonerspuddle, Moreton, Dorset."

On Tuesday 21 May 1935, two days after Lawrence's death, the coroner for East Dorset, Ralph Neville Jones, convened an inquest in the court-room at Bovington Military Hospital. Lawrence's body lay under its Union Jack in the nearby mortuary chapel. Thirty people were present and in his opening remarks Neville Jones told the jury they were considering the demise of a national hero: "Gentlemen of the Jury – I much regret the necessity for calling you together today to enquire into the circumstances leading up to the death of a very gallant Officer known at the time of his death as Thomas Edward Shaw, but better known to the world in general as Colonel Lawrence of Arabia.

"Despite the skill and devotion of the eminent Medical men who attended him and the Hospital Staff he died on Sunday last. When you have heard the evidence it will be for you to bring in your verdict.

"As to the actual cause of death you will have the evidence of Captain Allen the Army Specialist who with Mr Cairns conducted a post mortem examination and therefore on this point your verdict will be in accordance with the medical evidence."

The force of impact of the crash had been such that fragments of Lawrence's overalls were found embedded in the tarmacadam of the road. H. W. B. Cairns, the top London brain surgeon who sped across from his home at Arundel to advise on the last desperate attempt at saving Lawrence's life, had instead conducted a post mortem. There were such severe lacerations to the brain that a proper recovery would have been impossible and some at least of the body's motor functions would have been impaired.

Charles Philip Allen stated:

"I am a Captain in the Royal Army Medical Corps.

"At about 11.45 a.m. on the 13th May 1935 the Deceased Mr T. E. Shaw and Hargraves were both admitted to the Hospital at Bovington.

"I quickly examined Hargraves and found he was not seriously injured. At this time Mr Shaw was being carried up to the Theatre.

"I then examined Mr Shaw and found him deeply unconscious.

"I came to the conclusion he was suffering from severe head injuries. I had the skull x-rayed which showed a fracture.

"The Deceased remained unconscious until his death at 8 a.m. on the 19th

May 1935.

"With consent of the relatives I made a post mortem examination in conjunction with Mr Cairns.

"We found a large fissured fracture 9 inches long extending from the left side of the head backwards to the middle line – across the back of the skull and forward to the right side. Also small fracture of the orbital plate. The brain was very severely lacerated especially on the left side.

"Prior to death congestion of the lungs had set in and heart failure.

"In my opinion the cause of death was fracture of the skull and laceration of the brain, heart failure and congestion of the lungs.

"Had Mr Shaw lived he would have been unable to speak and would (have) lost his memory and would have been paralysed."

The circumstances of the crash were detailed by the two young cyclists, Albert Hargraves having been released temporarily into the court-room from his adjoining hospital bedroom, and they told the same story. Frank Fletcher additionally recalled seeing three pennies lying on the road, and asking Hargraves if they were his, with which the latter passed out. It is a telling little remark. Even in total shock we can be more outwardly troubled about the ownership of a silly bit of money than the chaos that is happening around us, such is the conditioning one receives from shortly after birth.

Frank Fletcher stated:

"I live at 50 Elles Road, Bovington Camp, and I am 14 years of age.

"On 13th May 1935 at about 11.20 a.m. I was riding a pedal bicycle from Bovington Camp towards Clouds Hill and Albert Hargraves was with me.

"I was riding in front and Hargraves was riding at the back.

"I was riding on the left of the road.

"When opposite Clouds Hill Camp I heard a motor-cycle coming up from behind. I then heard a crash and Bert's bicycle fell on top of me and knocked me off my bicycle. I got up and saw Mr Lawrence go over the handle bars of the motor-cycle and fall about 5 yards in front.

"I went to Bert who gave me his butchers' book and I saw 3 pennies lying on the road. He then seemed to fall asleep.

"I saw a lot of men running over from the tents."

Cross-examined by the Police: "There were no cars on the road then. I did not pass a car from the time I left Bovington Camp and the accident."

Cross-examined by the Jury: "We did not leave the road at all."

Cross-examined by Mr Ridge [on behalf of Hargraves's employer]: "I was riding close to the left hand side – between one and two yards."

Cross-examined by Mr Arnold Lawrence: "When the crash occurred the other boy was not at my side.

"I do not know what part of the road the motor-cyclist was on at the time of the accident.

"After Bert's bicycle struck me I looked up and saw the motor-cycle about 5 yards in front in the direction in which I was going and the rider going over the handle bars.

"We had been riding one behind the other for about 100 yards."

The words of the only independent witness who was called to give evidence, Corporal Ernest Catchpole, I have already partially quoted. He raised the question of the black car – both of the boys denied there was any other vehicle on the road. Irrespective of that, it was clear that with or without the appearance of a black car something had caused the inattention or loss of control of Lawrence's motor-cycle, which was little damaged. It had been examined and no obvious mechanical fault was apparent.

Corporal No 7581979 Ernest Catchpole of the Royal Army Ordnance Corps, stationed at Tidworth, stated:

"At about 11.20 a.m. on May 13th 1935 I was at Clouds Hill Camping Ground and about 100 yards from the road.

"I heard the noise of a motor-cycle coming from the direction of Bovington Camp. I saw the motor-cycle which was going between 50 and 60 miles and hour.

"Just before the motor-cycle got level with the Camp it passed a black car – it was a private car and the motor-cycle passed that safely. I then saw the motor-cyclist swerve across the road to avoid two pedal cyclists going in the same direction. The motor-cyclist swerved immediately after he passed the car which was going in the opposite direction.

"I then heard a crash and saw the motor-cycle twisting and turning over and over along the road.

"I immediately went to the road and called for help.

"I found the motor-cyclist lying on the right side of the road – his face was covered in blood and I sent to the Camp for a stretcher.

"An Army lorry came along and I asked them to take the injured persons to Hospital which they did.

"One of the pedal-cyclists was lying some distance down the road on the left side.

"I did not actually see the accident happen."

Cross-examined by Police Inspector Drake: "The car was not going very fast. I actually saw the deceased pass the car.

"I should say the collision occurred about 15 to 20 feet after the motor cyclist had passed the car."

Cross-examined by the Jury: "I do not know whether the pedal-cyclists were riding one behind the other or abreast.

"There would have been sufficient room for the motor-cyclist to pass between the car and the pedal-cyclists if the motor-cyclist had not been going at such a speed."

Cross-examined by Mr Ridge [for Hargraves's employer]: "I did not see the pedal-cyclists before the crash.

Cross-examined by Mr Arnold Lawrence: "The car was on its proper side of the road."

The injured bicyclist, Albert Hargraves, stated: "I am 14 years of age and live at 56b Somme Road, Bovington Camp. I am employed as an errand boy by Dodge & Co, Butchers, Bovington Camp.

"On 13th May 1935 I was cycling from Bovington Camp to Warwick [?; Waddock, surely] Cross, Tonerspuddle [Turners Puddle] and Frank Fletcher was with me for company.

"Opposite Clouds Hill Camp I was riding 4 or 5 feet behind Fletcher and on the left hand side of the road. I heard the sound of a motor-cycle coming from behind.

"No motor car passed me about this time nor any traffic of any sort.

"I do not remember any more until I found myself in Hospital. I do not even remember being thrown off my bicycle." This had a smashed back wheel and the coroner drew attention to the size of its frame. It was, he felt, too big for Hargraves. The boy was particularly questioned about the position of the two bicycles. "We were in single-file for about 80 yards," he said. Hargraves was then taken outside to check his idea of distance and described that between the court room and a telegraph pole as being about 80 yards, with which nobody seemed to disagree.

Cross-examined by the Jury: "We were not talking."

Cross-examined by Mr Arnold Lawrence: "We had been riding one behind the other for about 10 minutes.

"We were riding at a normal pace with both hands on the handlebars. The bicycle is the right size for me but I have to reach a little for the pedals.

"We changed positions because of the noise of the motor-cycle.

"We had been riding in single file for about 80 yards."

Cross-examined by Police Inspector Drake: "When we left Bovington Camp we were riding abreast."

Cross-examined by Mr Arnold Lawrence: "I slowed up and got behind Frank. I did not wobble at all. The road was not uneven at the side where I was riding."

No one made a point about the bicyclists being hidden in a dip in the road because all the evidence was that they were not – they were moving and had been visible approaching the brow of the hill fifteen seconds before the impact. Anything to the contrary is from the mountain of subsequent misinformation. Those at the inquest formed the clear impression that Lawrence had hurtled into something he should have seen. This is absolutely clear not only from what the journalists wrote but also from the coroner's summing up. No one suggested Lawrence had ridden into a hidden hazard – that was the whole point they were puzzling over. He had instead gone into an accident where the hazard was visible and avoidable. It should have been as trivial and uneventful as countless thousands of other such manoeuvres he had successfully accomplished in the past. For some inexplicable reason, however, it was different.

The Dorset County Chronicle reporter commented: "Those who knew

Lawrence knew such a brilliant motor-cyclist even though he was travelling at 50 to 60 m.p.h. would never crash aimlessly into a cyclist unless he was faced with a last second difficulty in his path."

The coroner began his summing up:

"The only conflicting point in the evidence seems to be that with regard to the car. I do not necessarily mean that the car had anything to do with the accident but the fact that Corporal Catchpole is certain that he saw it and the boys are certain that they did not is rather unsatisfactory."

These important sentences do not appear in the official report of Inquisition No.160 but were taken down by reporters.

There was but one conclusion towards which Neville Jones had to direct his jury of seven, who included soldiers: "You have now heard the evidence and I do not think you will have any difficulty in arriving at your verdict.

"The facts are only too clear and that the collision was an accident there can be no doubt, what caused the Deceased to run into the pedal-cyclist from the rear we shall never know, but the evidence would lead one to think that Mr Shaw must have been travelling at a very fast speed and possibly lost control of his motor-cycle.

"I do not think there can be any other conclusion on the evidence.

"Under the circumstances you will doubtless consider the proper verdict to bring in will be one of accidental death."

Verdict: "Died from injuries received accidentally."

Neville Jones then brought the inquest to its close: "Needless to say, I entirely concur in your verdict and I am sure you would wish me to convey your sympathy as well as my own to Mr Shaw's relatives in the loss they and our country have sustained through the untimely death of such a gallant Englishman."

The newsreels had coined another phrase. Lawrence was "the mystery man of the twentieth century".

The official record of the inquest concludes more prosaically: "AN INQUISITION taken for our Sovereign Lord the King, at the Military Hospital, Bovington Camp, in the Parish of Wool in the Eastern District of the County of Dorset on the 21st day of May 1935, before Ralph Neville Jones Esquire, one of the Coroners of our said Lord the King, for the said County of Dorset upon the Oath of seven good and lawful Men of the said Parish of Wool duly sworn to inquire for our said Lord the King, touching the death of Thomas Edward Shaw and upon view of his body (by me) and those of the said Jurors whose names are hereto subscribed, upon their Oaths do say:

"That the said Thomas Edward Shaw whilst riding a motor-cycle between Bovington Camp and Clouds Hill, Tonerspuddle [Turners Puddle], at 11.30 a.m. on the 13th May 1935 collided with a pedal-cyclist. He was thrown from his machine and sustained serious injury, and died at the Military Hospital on the 19th May 1935 without recovering consciousness, and that the cause of his death was congestion of the lungs and heart failure following a fracture of the skull and laceration of the brain sustained as aforesaid, and so do further say that the said Thomas Edward Shaw by accident came to his death as aforesaid and the Jurors aforesaid, do further say that the said Thomas Edward Shaw was a male person of the age of forty-six years, and a Retired Aircraftman residing at Clouds Hill in the parish of Tonerspuddle in the County of Dorset.

"In Witness whereof as well the said Coroner as the Jurors have hereunder subscribed their Hands and Seals this 21st day of May 1935. R. Neville Jones (Coroner). S. C. Patrick (Foreman). Jesse Rawles, G. Mason, R. Dulleston, W. G. Cluff (?), M. White (?), Thomas Shaw."

County of Dorset - Eastern District

Inquest No 160

Dated 21st May 1935

DEPOSITIONS

taken at the Inquest on view of the body of Thomas Edward Shaw of Clouds Hill Tonerspuddle Moreton Dorset.

VERDICT

No. 160.

Dated 21st May 1935

Inquisition

taken on View of the Body of Thomas Edward Shaw of Clouds Hill Tonerspuddle Moreton Dorset sometime known as Colonel Lawrence of Arabia.

Verdict:

Congestion of Lungs and Heart failure following a fracture of the Skull and laceration of the brain sustained upon being thrown from his Motor Cycle when colliding with a pedal Cyclist. Accidental death R.N.

Coroners 8.

Shaw & Sons Ltd., Fetter Lane, E.C.4 J131 & L130 81435 (0)

Eastern District
County of Dorset
to wit.

An Inquisition

taken for our Sovereign Lord the King, at The Military Hospital Bovington Camp in the Parish of Wool in the County of Dorset on the 21st day of May 1935 [and by adjournment on the ~~day of~~ ~~and the~~ ~~day of~~], before Ralph Neville Jones Esquire, one of the Coroners of our said Lord the King, for the said County of Dorset upon the Oath of seven of good and lawful Men of the said Parish of Wool duly sworn to inquire for our said Lord the King, touching the death of Thomas Edward Shaw and upon view of his body [by me] and those of the said Jurors whose names are hereunto subscribed, upon their Oaths do say:—

That the said Thomas Edward Shaw whilst riding a motor cycle between Bovington Camp and Clouds Hill Tonerspuddle at 11·30 am on the 13th May 1935 collided with a pedal cyclist. He was thrown from his machine and sustained serious injury, and died at the Military Hospital on the 19th May 1935 without regaining consciousness. and that the cause of his death was Congestion of the Lungs and Heart failure following a fracture of the Skull and Laceration of the brain sustained as aforesaid.

and so do further say that the said Thomas Edward Shaw by accident came to his death as aforesaid

and the Jurors aforesaid, do further say that the said Thomas Edward Shaw was a male person of the age of forty six years, and a Retired Aircraftsman residing at Clouds Hill in the parish of Tonerspuddle in the County of Dorset

In Witness whereof as well the said Coroner as the Jurors have hereunder subscribed their Hands and Seals this 21st day of May 1935

R. Neville Jones (Coroner.)
Foreman P.L. Patrick
Jesse Rawles
[illegible] Gleason
R Dullerton
[illegible]
[illegible]
Thos. Shaw

Address by the Coroner to the Jury.

Gentlemen of the Jury - I much regret the necessity for calling you together today to enquire into the circumstances leading up to the death of a very gallant Officer known at the time of his death as Thomas Edward Shaw, but better known to the world in general as Colonel Lawrence of Arabia.

Despite the skill and devotion of the eminent Medical men who attended him and the Hospital Staff he died on Sunday last. When you have heard the evidence it will be for you to bring in your verdict.

As to the actual cause of death you will have the evidence of Captain Allen the Army Specialist who with Mr Cairns conducted a post mortem examination and therefore on this point your verdict will be in accordance with the medical evidence.

You have now heard the evidence and I do not think you will have any difficulty in arriving at your verdict.

The facts are only too clear and that the collision was an accident there can be no doubt, what caused the Deceased to run into the pedal cyclist from the rear we shall never know, but the evidence would lead one to think that Mr. Shaw must have been travelling at a very fast speed and possibly lost control of his motor cycle.

I do not think there can be any other conclusion on the evidence.

Under the circumstances you will doubtless consider the proper verdict to bring in will be one of accidental death.

After the Jury had returned a verdict of accidental death, the Coroner added.

Needless to say I entirely concur in your verdict and I am sure you would wish me to convey your sympathy as well as my own to Mr. Shaw's relatives in the loss they and our country has sustained through the untimely death of such a gallant Englishman.

INQUEST NO 160.

County of Dorset)
Eastern District)
to wit)

INFORMATION OF WITNESSES severally taken and acknowledged on behalf of our Sovereign Lord the King touching the death of Thomas Edward Shaw (aged 46 years) of Clouds Hill Tonerspuddle Moreton at The Military Hospital Bovington Camp in the County of Dorset this 21st day of May 1935 before me RALPH NEVILLE JONES one of his Majesty's Coroners for the said County of Dorset on view of the body of the said person then and there lying dead.

Mr G.T. Ridge appears on behalf of the employer of the boy Hargraves.

Arnold Walter Lawrence

I live at 31 Madingley Road Cambridge and I am a brother of the Deceased.

I identify the body viewed by the Coroner as that of Thomas Edward Shaw. Since March last the Deceased had resided at Clouds Hill Tonerspuddle.

The name of the Deceased was formerly Thomas Edward Lawrence and he changed it by Deed Poll.

The Deceased was a single man and his age was 46 or 47. & a retired ~~army officer~~ Aircraftsman. A.W.L.

A.W. Lawrence

Corporal No 7581979 Ernest Catchpole
R.A.O.C. stationed at Tidworth states:-
At about 11.30 am on May
13th 1935 I was at Clouds Hill
Camping Ground & about 100
yards from the road.
I heard the noise of a motor
cycle coming from the direction
of Bovington Camp. I saw
the motorcycle which was going
between 50 & 60 miles an hour.
Just before the motorcycle got
level with the Camp it passed
a black car – it was a private
car & the motorcycle passed that
safely. I then saw the motor
cyclist swerve across the road
to avoid two pedal cyclists going
in the same direction. The motor
cyclist swerved immediately after
he passed the car which was
going in the opposite direction.
I then heard a crash and
saw the motor cycle twisting & turning
over & over along the road.
I immediately went to the
road & called for help ~~…~~.
I found the motorcyclist lying
on the right side of the road – his
face was covered in blood & I
sent to the Camp for a stretcher.
An army lorry came along
& I asked them to take the injured
persons to Hospital which they did.

One of the pedal cyclists was lying some distance down the road on the left side.

I did not actually see the accident happen.

By the Police — The car was not going very fast. I actually saw the Deceased pass the car.

I should say the collision occurred about 15 to 20 feet after the motor cyclist had passed the car.

By the Jury — I do not know whether the pedal cyclists were riding one behind the other or abreast.

There would have been sufficient room for the motor cyclist to pass between the car & the pedal cyclists if the motor cyclist had not been going at such a speed.

By Mr Ridge — I did not see the pedal cyclists before the crash.

By Mr Lawrence — The car was on its proper side of the road.

Hatchard

Albert Hargraves states:-

I am 14 years of age & live at 5b6 Somme Road Bovington Camp. I am employed as an errand boy by Dodge & Co Butchers Bovington Camp.

On 13th May 1935 I was cycling from Bovington Camp to Warwick Cross Tonnerspuddle & Frank Fletcher was with me for company.

Opposite Clouds Hill Camp I was riding 4 to 5 feet behind Fletcher & on the left hand side of the road. I heard the sound of a motorcycle coming from behind.

No motor car passed me about this time nor any traffic of any sort.

I do not remember any more until I found myself in Hospital

Cross-examined

By the Jury We were not talking.

By Mr Lawrence We had been riding one behind the other for about 10 minutes

We were riding at a normal pace with both hands on the handlebars. The bicycle is the right size for me but I have to reach a little for the pedals.

We changed positions because of the noise of the motorcycle

We had been riding in single

file for about 80 yards.

By the Police: When we left Bovington Camp we were riding abreast

By Mr Lawrence: I slowed up & got behind Frank
I did not wobble at all.
The road was not uneven at the side where I was riding.

Albert Hargraves..

Frank Fletcher, states:- I live at 50 Lilles Road Bovington Camp & I am 14 years of age.

On 13th May 1935 at about 11.20 a.m. I was riding a pedal bicycle from Bovington Camp towards Clouds Hill & Albert Hargraves was with me.

I was riding in front and Hargraves was riding at the back.

I was riding on the left of the road.

When opposite Clouds Hill Camp I heard a motorcycle coming up from behind - I then heard a crash and Bert's bicycle fell on top of me & knocked me off my bicycle. I got up & saw Mr Lawrence go over the handle bars of the motorcycle & fall about 5 yards in front.

I went to Bert who gave me his butchers book & I saw 3 pennies lying on the road. He then seemed to fall asleep.

I saw a lot of men running over from the tents.

Cross-examined By the Police — There were no cars on the road then. I did not pass a car from the time I left Bovington Camp ~~until~~ and the accident.

By the Jury — We did not leave the road at all.

By Mr Ledge — I was riding close to the left hand side - between one & two yards.

By Mr Lawrence — When the crash occurred the other boy was not at my side
I do not know ~~where he was~~ what part of the road the motor cyclist was on at the time of the accident.

After Bert's bicycle struck me I looked up & saw the motor cycle about 5 yards in front in the direction in which I was going & the rider going over the handle bars
We had been riding one behind the other for about 100 yards

Frank Fletcher

Charles Philip Allen states :-
I am a Captain in the R.A.M.C.
at about 11.45 a.m. on the
13th May 1935 the Deceased Mr
T. E. Shaw & Hargraves were both
admitted to the Hospital at Bovington
I ~~fou~~ quickly examined Hargraves
& found he was not seriously injured.
At this time Mr Shaw was being
carried up to the Theatre.
I then examined Mr Shaw
& found him deeply unconscious.
I came to the conclusion that
he was suffering from severe
head injuries. I had the Skull
~~ex~~ rayed which showed a fracture.
The Deceased remained unconscious
until his death at 8 a.m. on the
19th May 1935.
With consent of the relatives
I made a post mortem examination
in conjunction with Mr Cairns -
^before^ A large fissured fracture
9 inches long extending from the
left side of the head backwards
to the middle line - across the
back of the Skull & forward to the
right side. Also small fracture
of left orbital plate. The brain
was very severely lacerated
especially on the left side
Prior to death congestion of
the lungs had set in & heart failure
In my opinion the cause

of death was fracture of the skull
& laceration of the brain heart
failure & congestion of the lungs.
Had Mr Shaw lived he would
have been unable to speak & would
lost his memory & would have been
paralyzed.

[illegible signature]

Mechanical failure considered

Mechanically, a lot of rubbish has been printed about the capabilities of the Brough Superior. For instance, the statement by Knightley and Simpson in *Secret Lives of Lawrence of Arabia* – repeated by Desmond Stewart in his *T. E. Lawrence* – that it could only have managed 38 m.p.h. in second gear, this being the gear in which it was apparently jammed during the accident. The machine has three gears. In second it would go flat-out at 50 m.p.h. plus. In top it would pull away from 30 m.p.h. to in excess of 100 m.p.h.

Not for nothing did it gain a reputation as "the Rolls-Royce of motor-cycles". Had Lawrence indeed dropped down to second gear just before the impact he could still have been moving at between 50 and 60 m.p.h. as the inquest heard.

Colin Graham's article in the second issue of Dorset County Magazine led Frank Parsons of Hyde, near Fordingbridge, to provide information of a mechanical failure to another Brough Superior motor-cycle in the 1930s: "I remember, a year or two after Lawrence's death I met a young man in Brighton who was rebuilding a Brough Superior after a crash which had some similarity to the one described in your article; fortunately without fatal consequences. I learned that he, with his brother riding pillion, was travelling at about 60 m.p.h. on the straight road from Ditchling to Brighton, and slowing for the corner at the foot of Clayton Hill, when the front brake seized (or jammed) with disastrous result.

"Corporal Catchpole's description of Lawrence's crash, 'I saw the bike turning and twisting over and over along the road', would aptly describe the accident at Clayton. This possible explanation of the accident at Bovington, although less romantic, is I suggest, the more likely."

Lawrence, who never wore a crash-helmet, was in the view of his motor-cycle's maker, George Brough, "One of the finest riders I have ever met. In the several runs I took with him, I am able to state that T.E.L. was most considerate to every other road user. I never saw him take a single risk nor put any other rider or driver to the slightest inconvenience."

George Brough's 'black paint'

The balance of probability in respect of the inquest witnesses, with the conflict of evidence between Corporal Catchpole and the boys, might have been regarded differently if motor-cycle manufacturer George Brough had given evidence.

He had been called to check over GW 2275 two hours after the accident and though there was no structural or mechanical fault he noted black paint on the offside handlebar and petrol tank.

Howard Dodsworth of Tunbridge Wells, who had spoken to Brough's widow, Conny, confirmed this to Colin Graham in 1978, with the comment that George Brough was "unwilling to perjure himself" and would have felt compelled to mention the motor-cycle's impact with a black object had he been summoned to give evidence.

He believed to his dying day that his expert evidence had been suppressed and that there was therefore more to the otherwise inexplicable crash than the authorities would admit.

Lawrence's own evidence: positioning his motor-cycle

As the jigsaw falls into some sort of picture my gut reaction is that the security services, and MI5 in particular, were closely watching Lawrence for two reasons. Firstly they were naturally suspicious of anyone who was likely to be placed above them in a reorganisation that at the very least would be resented and inconvenient. They also had a duty to monitor the current liaisons and outlook of a man who might become the overlord of Britain's entire intelligence operations.

Lawrence's death is a mystery. Two boys were adamant that one of Britain's fastest and most experienced motor-cyclists careered into them from the rear on a straight and empty road with at least twelve feet of clearance. The single onlooker to be questioned was equally insistent that the crash had taken place immediately after Lawrence had cleared a black car that had come along the road from the opposite direction. What he saw, or thought he had seen, tormented this witness for the rest of his life. Something was to put him in such despair that he put a bullet through his brain as he lay in his bunk in the Western Desert in the Second World War.

I was going to avoid the issue of which piece of the conflicting evidence I believed. Then I realised that Lawrence himself had decided it for me. He would not have ridden into the back of a pair of cyclists whom he had seen from about half a mile away if he had not been forced by some other consideration into positioning his motor-cycle close to the nearside edge of the road. He had also apparently changed down to the middle of the motor-cycle's three gears. The positioning, however, is the crucial piece of silent evidence. One does that for a single obvious reason – oncoming traffic.

Therefore, for whatever reason – inattention or distraction from the new summer camp they were passing – the fact that the boys did not notice a black car is not as convincing in evidence as the angle of approach of the motor-cycle. That, for me, clinches the fact that there was something substantial in the form of oncoming traffic and I have attended enough inquests as a reporter to know that witnesses such as Corporal Ernest Catchpole do not invent wild stories for no possible motive or advantage, in fact only disadvantage as the statements of the boys were bound to devalue everything he said. If there had been any doubt in his mind, his ordeal as a witness could have been eased by simply agreeing to their story.

What we cannot know, nor even the boys themselves, is just who was talking to them in the days between the crash and the inquest. MI5 put a security screen around Bovington, that extended to the neighbouring post offices at Moreton and Wool, as Lawrence lay dying. The closest functioning telegraph office was at the back of the grocery shop at Crossways, between Affpuddle and Warmwell. Dorothy Meech, who ran the local carrier service into Dorchester for the villagers, wrote to Colin Graham at the Dorset County Magazine:

"A Mrs Stapleton ran a general grocery shop, I believe it is still there, and sub post office at Crossways. She was rung up one morning by the postmistress from Moreton asking her to take the telegrams and messages as the Moreton telephone was out of order. The press were becoming interested."

Two nurses from Bournemouth cared for Lawrence as he lay dying in Bovington Military Hospital. They also were kept in ignorance, the Daily Sketch reported on 20 May: "The name of the injured man was not then revealed, and the nurses were ordered to keep silent. Yesterday the nurses returned to Bournemouth, but could say nothing. Until they saw the newspapers they did not know who the patient was – beyond the fact that his name was Shaw."

That the black car was not located is consistent with someone not wanting it to be found. It was, after all, one of the most highly publicised road accidents of the century. I do not see the handling of Lawrence's crash investigation as an ordinary piece of policing. Its controllers were the nation's political policemen. What was revealed therefore, eye-witness Catchpole excepted, was what the authorities wished to be revealed.

My opinion, for what little it is worth, is that on the balance of probabilities there was a black car, the driver of which had some motive for not coming forward to assist the inquiries because something it did caused the motor-bike and – or – its rider to go totally out of control. The rest can be left almost unsaid, apart from pointing out that the stream of subsequent revelations would have made it impossible for Lawrence to clear 1980s-style positive security vetting. Not that unusual habits preclude people from being national heroes. Nor, indeed does straight, conformist heterosexuality ensure that an individual will be brave and loyal for his country.

The unsuitability of T. E. Lawrence to head the security services in those changing times was his mental flirtation with the country's leading neo-Nazi intellectual, Henry Williamson. Make no mistake about grasping this point: the British Union of Fascists in 1935 had moved on from simply endorsing the Italian political system – it was now Adolf Hitler's English supporters' club.

Lawrence was no more acceptable to the operatives of the security service as their overall commander than the Prince of Wales was fit to be King Edward VIII. In both cases personal magnetism was offset by indiscretion and a certain real or imagined sympathy towards the new Germany. Prince Edward would succeed his father in 1936 and become the first bachelor King for 176 years: though his desire to change that situation contained the seed for his destruction and the establishment was in no mood for any compromise that might enable him to remain King. It was as the Duke of Windsor, in 1937, that he visited Germany and met Hitler, Goebbels and Goering.

A system that can connive to remove its King would have been well able to block the further progress of Colonel T. E. Lawrence. Whether there was an assassination or merely an unfortunate and fatal accident to the subject during the course of surveillance I am undecided. That these, however, were the circumstances I am beyond doubting.

Talking to David Radcliff of the Dorset Evening Echo, for a report that appeared on 4 January 1986, Mrs Margaret Montague of Wimborne said "there definitely was a car, and it was a black one". It was a Hillman, driven by her late husband, Lionel Montague, who died in about 1970. The registration was COW 41, a Southampton number-plate.

Mrs Montague said that Lionel had passed Lawrence immediately before the accident: "The driver and Lawrence waved to each other." They were acquainted it seems, from stopping at the same garages, such as Sandford, for petrol: "My husband was six foot three. Lawrence looked so small by his side. He was not a very distinguished looking man, Mr Lawrence."

The Montagues were living in Poole and Lionel was an insurance company manager. Later on the day of Lawrence's crash he pulled in to the Sandford Service Station and was told of the accident. "I don't think so – because I've just waved to him!" he replied. "It must have happened seconds after my husband waved to him," Mrs Montague added. "He had told me before that that bike would be the death of Mr Shaw. It was an awful looking thing, sinister looking."

I am not wholly convinced, because the memory tends to telescope events and he could well have seen Lawrence a little earlier in the day on his way into Bovington Camp from Clouds Hill. On the other hand the distraction of a car would be an ingredient for the otherwise inexplicable inattention that resulted in such a proficient motor-cyclist ploughing into a pair of boy bicyclists. It also begs the question of why Lionel Montague did not come forward with his evidence – this being one of the best publicised road accidents of all time – and raises the possibility of his car having received a glancing blow from an off-balance Lawrence.

If Lawrence had spun into difficulties at that moment the driver could well have been completely unaware of the predicament and disaster that was unfolding to his rear. To accept this as the explanation one would have to disregard motor-cycle manufacturer George Brough and his suppressed evidence of black paint of an actual impact.

Bovington's butcher recalled the events of the crash

The Lawrence recollections industry has since worked overtime with second-generation hearsay but in the 1960s some of the key people were still alive.

Bill Bugg told me in 1968 that he had been one of the seven jurymen at the inquest – which he wasn't – and was the last to see Lawrence alive, as he came out of the ironmonger's at Bovington Camp with a paint-brush which he said was for the window-frames at Clouds Hill.

F. J. Stratton wrote to the Dorset County Magazine office from 11 Rectory Grove, off Lodge Road in Winson Green, Birmingham. "I lived in Bovington from 1934 to 1957," he told us, "and during part of that time I had a butcher's shop, just opposite the Post Office. On the Monday morning [13 May 1935] I had sent my errand boy, Albert Hargraves, around to get orders. About 11 o'clock Lawrence (Shaw) motor-cycled down from his house to the Post Office to collect his mail, which was always tied up and sealed as secret news.

"He came to the shop as he had done many times when home here, to buy two chops for his lunch. After a short chat he remarked he must be going as he had to report to Catterick [Catterick Garrison, North Yorkshire] at 5 pm that day on his very powerful motor-cycle – some travelling.

"On reaching the place where my errand boy had got to, for some unknown reason he collided with the black wheel of his cycle, knocking this some twenty yards into the bushes and brambles on his side of the road. Lawrence, by the impact, must have lost his balance as the footrest had ploughed the road up quite deep for about thirty yards and finally lost control and came right off, his head striking a large stone placed on the edge of the road. I have a portion of the cycle handle and a piece of his coat he was wearing, cut right out of his shoulder as large as a plate.

"The bicycle was quite a wreck and Hargraves was very much knocked about and bruised. News came to the camp in no time and the ambulance brought Lawrence and my boy back down to the hospital. I visited the hospital several times to enquire and see Hargraves but Lawrence was very badly hurt and the doctor told me there was no hope to save him. I attended the inquest, at the hospital, but very little evidence was given, as it all seemed a hush-hush affair. His brother and a solicitor attended. He was placed in a mortuary in a very rough plain coffin and just a black name-plate.

"I attended the funeral at Moreton church and the burial in the cemetery. His wish was for no flowers, but there was a rough wooden cross with a daffodil on it from the lady whom he lodged with previously. The grave was filled in and the cross, bearing an Arabic word meaning 'Peace', and the daffodil were left, but at four o'clock it had been stolen, by souvenir hunters, I expect.

"The road was in fair condition when the accident happened. My errand boy had 3 feet 6 inches and Lawrence 18 feet to go by him [others say 12]; so something went wrong by someone.

"The only reason I can suggest is that just opposite where the accident happened soldiers were putting up tents for a summer camp, and taking his attention he lost direction for a few seconds. Going the speed he always rode at, the crash was a bad one. Hargraves was in hospital six weeks, newspaper reporters were all at the camp, but all news was suppressed for three days."

Churchill's hopes, and the Moreton funeral

Winston Churchill, who came down to Moreton to lead the procession at Lawrence's funeral, gave an eulogy to the press on 19 May that firmly linked him with the gathering storm in world politics and the fact that Lawrence was destined for a rôle: "We have lost one of the greatest beings of our time. I hoped to see him quit his retirement and take a commanding part in facing the dangers which now threaten the country." That part, I contend, was the leadership of a re-structured secret intelligence service.

The funeral took place in the afternoon of Tuesday 21 May 1935, in the parish church of St Nicholas beside the River Frome at Moreton. Not everyone approved. "What about Westminster Abbey?", George Bernard Shaw had snapped in Durban, according to Reuter's news agency. "His country, which refused to give him a small pension, owes him at least a stone." Lawrence wanted otherwise; no mourning, no flowers, and no military colour party.

After the inquest, a Bournemouth-registered hearse carried the body from Bovington to Moreton. The little village of thatched cottages nestling in the shades of tall trees was hosting the biggest invasion of local, national and international visitors Dorset had seen. Three special coaches had carried mourners down the London and South Western Railway from Waterloo. Major-General Archibald Percival Wavell, who was with the Egyptian Expeditionary Force in 1917–20, upstaged them by arriving from Aldershot in an experimental autogyro. It was, I think, the first helicopter to be seen in the Dorset sky. Some 170 packed the church with hundreds left thronging outside.

The church's guide book claims George Bernard Shaw was among those who made the trip, but South Africa to south Dorset in three days was an

Sir John Salmond, Marshal of the Royal Air Force, attended Lawrence's funeral. He and his brother were among Lawrence's closest and most influential friends. The brother, Air Chief Marshal Sir Geoffrey Salmond, had died in 1933.

Lawrence's exit from Bovington Camp and Winston Churchill's grim arrival at Moreton church to pay the nation's last respects to 'one of the greatest beings of our time'. Overleaf, and hatless, Churchill is seen leading the main concourse of mourners out of the church and along the lane to the village cemetery. Ahead of them, also pictured overleaf, Lawrence's coffin was wheeled on a trolley.

impossibility in the 1930s. Those who were able to make the journey included Atta Bey Amin (chargé d'affaires, Iraq Legation); Lady Astor (Nancy Astor, the first woman to take her seat as an MP); Jonathan Cape (his publisher); Lionel Curtis (global affairs expert, who bought Lawrence's gold-hafted dagger); Robert Graves (poet and author); Mrs Florence Hardy (the novelist's widow); Basil Liddell Hart (military biographer); Augustus John (artist); Lord Lloyd (former High Commissioner for Egypt); Sir John Salmond (Marshal of the Royal Air Force); and Siegfried Sassoon (Great War Infantry officer and poet).

One psalm was chanted, number cxxxi: "I will lift up mine eyes unto the hills."

They sang one hymn. "Jesu, Lover of my Soul" was said to have been Lawrence's favourite, but then they were bound to say that.

From the church Lawrence's coffin was wheeled two hundred yards out to the village burial ground on the west side of the lane towards Wool [Ordnance Survey map reference SY 804 893]. His plot is in the second row from the back – go straight ahead from the gate and it is then to your right.

Six pall-bearers pushed or flanked the trolley: Aircraftman W. Bradbury (friend from the sea-plane project); Arthur Russell (Royal Tank Corps friend); Eric Kennington (illustrator of *Seven Pillars of Wisdom* and the man who would carve his effigy); Pat Knowles (Lawrence's local helper, who with his wife Joyce lived in the chalet bungalow on the west side of the road at Clouds Hill and would look after Lawrence's home for the National Trust); Colonel S. F. Newcombe (comrade from the Desert Revolt); and Sir Ronald Storrs (Governor of Jerusalem, 1917–20).

Winston Churchill did not hide his tears at the graveside. With Lawrence, a memento of Arabia went into the ground: grass from Akaba had been placed in his coffin. As the dust was scattered a sole floral tribute appeared, of lilac and forget-me-nots, bearing a Lyme Regis hotel label with the message: "To T.E.L. who should sleep among kings."

For his brother Arnold there were dozens of messages of sympathy. King George V conveyed the national grief: "The King has heard with sincere regret of the death of your brother and deeply sympathises with you and your family in this sad loss. Your brother's name will live in history, and the King gratefully recognises his distinguished services to his country, and feels that it is tragic that the end should have come in this manner to a life still so full of promise."

Most of the mourners had heard the tribute on the wireless from Field-Marshal Viscount Allenby, the Commander-in-Chief of the Egyptian

Last glimpses into the open grave at Moreton's village burying ground.

En route between Moreton church and cemetery — one of the photographers who followed Lawrence to the end.

Expeditionary Force which mounted the campaign against the Turks, which the B.B.C. was also broadcasting to the Empire. It was a soldier's farewell to a comrade: "He shared with the Arabs their hardships and dangers. Among these desert raiders there was none who would not have willingly died for his chief [meaning Lawrence]. He had a genius for leadership. Above all men he had no regard for ambition, but did his duty as he saw it."

Lord Lloyd, who was at the funeral in Moreton, brought a note of consolation and triumph to shine through the grief. It came from Britain's last great colonial administrator, George Ambrose Lloyd, who would go on to die in the job, as Colonial Secretary, in 1941. Lloyd said it for Lawrence himself, with a few beautiful words that no one was able to improve upon:

"He was one of those rare beings who seemed to belong to the morning of the world. His end would have pleased him – a swift rush and a sudden passing."

Seigfried Sassoon records a last dig at the press, on Lawrence's behalf, in his *Poet's Pilgrimage*:

"As I stood by T. E. Lawrence's open grave, a man tried to photograph the coffin. I knocked the camera out of his hands, God forgive me!"

Afterwards the principal dignitaries were given tea in Moreton House by Lady Findlay who was living there. She was the widow of the ambassador Sir Mansfield Findlay.

Before the erection of the stone, and before his mother even knew Lawrence had been buried, the grave was already a place of pilgrimage. When on Sunday 26 May 1935 a Dorset County Chronicle representative drew up in the lane beside Moreton House he found more than a score of motor-cars, and cyclists and hikers were also searching out the spot. Hundreds had already visited it. He reported on 30 May 1935:

"Outside the cemetery gates a Moreton woman was selling threepenny postcard photographs of funeral scenes. She said that she had sold more than 500 of them.

"At the funeral on Tuesday week only one floral tribute was placed on the grave. By Thursday, however, the mound was strewn with wild flowers picked from Moreton Heath and laid on the grave by visitors. There were rhododendrons, bluebells, campions, daisies, buttercups, forget-me-nots, and lilac.

"On Sunday these had been cleared away, and all the grave bore was a roughly-hewn cross, a tribute of the Temple of the Brave. It was placed there on the day of the funeral by a Southampton man, Mr W. H. Adams, who is warden of the Temple of the Brave."

Lawrence's mother, who had tried to convert the Chinese to Christianity with about as much lasting success as she had managed with her own inscrutable son, would give him a gravestone that firmly returned Lawrence to the academic world and her God. It was honest to her faith, but for him it would have been the same hypocrisy that he had so virulently denounced in the case of Dorset's other pillar of fame, by mocking Hardy's funeral arrangements. Indeed Lawrence had encouraged his political friends into action to abolish the compulsory military church parades which spoiled his Sundays.

The headstone reads:

TO THE DEAR MEMORY OF

T. E. LAWRENCE

FELLOW OF ALL SOVLS COLLEGE

OXFORD

BORN 16 AVGVST 1888

DIED 19 MAY 1935

THE HOVR IS COMING & NOW IS

WHEN THE DEAD SHALL HEAR

THE VOICE OF THE

SON OF GOD

AND THEY THAT HEAR

SHALL LIVE

The words on the open book at his feet, the motto of the Oxford University Press, are from the twenty-sixth Psalm:

DOMINVS ILLVMINATIO MEA

Had he lived, Churchill would have made Lawrence 'C'

Not only MI5 and the various counter-espionage agencies were under the threat of review in 1935. There was also the problem of what to do with MI6, which would come to a head on 9 November 1939 when two of its agents, Major Stevens and Captain Best, were kidnapped at Venlo by the German SS.

MI6 was otherwise known as the Secret Intelligence Service (SIS) – which reflected its overseas information gathering rôle – and more generally simply as the Secret Service. Its responsibility was, and is, all matters of security that are beyond the borders of the United Kingdom.

The head of the Secret Service at this time, 'C' as he was known, was Admiral Hugh "Quex" Sinclair. He had taken over from the first 'C' – Captain Smith-Cumming who on his one leg had charted MI6's course through the Great War. Sinclair's effective deputy was Colonel Stewart

In Moreton cemetery: no longer T. E. Shaw, the name he had legally acquired by deed poll, but back in his mother's missionary fold as one of God's academicians.

Menzies of the Life Guards, the head of MI6's Section V, who had been appointed by the Foreign Office in 1915. Headship of the Secret Service was regarded as a fiefdom of the Royal Navy, the Silent Service, but when Sinclair died of cancer in November 1939 the mould was broken at a meeting in No.10 Downing Street. Prime Minister Neville Chamberlain met with Lord Halifax, Winston Churchill and Sir Alexander Cadogan at 6.30

pm on 28 November 1939 and appointed Menzies to succeed Sinclair.

Menzies had to cope with a torrent of information that was beyond his abilities as he controlled the dissemination of the entire massive flow of intercepted German radio signals traffic from the Enigma coding machines, which the enemy wrongly considered impossible to decipher. It was his decision what the Prime Minister saw and what the R.A.F., the other military departments, and individual mortals needed to be told; and how in order to protect the precious Ultra Secret source the information would be disguised and presented. The Government Code and Cipher School, based at Bletchley Park in Hertfordshire, carried out the huge code-breaking operation and was responsible via MI6 to the Foreign Office.

If ... it is impossible to say what might have been ... but given Churchill's fascination for his Ultra insights into the enemy's mind and intentions, and his stated admiration for the equally complex computer that was the mind of T. E. Lawrence, I am sure that by the summer of 1940 Lawrence would have been 'C' and editing the great man's daily input of titbits revealing the

Eric Kennington sculpted the memorials of Dorset's heroes and worthies, with Thomas Hardy in bronze at Top o' Town, Dorchester, and T. E. Lawrence in stone at Wareham. Kennington is pictured in the Home Guard uniform of the coming conflict.

other side's plans in the world at war. It would have been the great finale, the supreme translation job of the century with every nuance hiding a greater secret – the source itself – in a manner in which Lawrence would have excelled. Here the little lies and the hidden truth could have been obscured into something that was neither fact nor fiction but a necessity in the game-plan to save the nation. It was the great job of the Second World War which Lawrence would have done so well; the last creative confinement of a career contained by huts.

Kennington's effigy of Lawrence, at Wareham

Eric Kennington, the illustrator of *Seven Pillars of Wisdom*, sculpted a bust of Lawrence for the crypt of St Paul's Cathedral and a life-sized effigy lying in classic mediaeval style in the rôle for which he is remembered, Lawrence of Arabia. There was discussion as to where it should go and Reverend Michael Kinloch, the rector of Moreton, was not going to have it in his church. He had heard sufficient of Lawrence's behaviour to question his Christian credentials and did not wish to see St Nicholas's church, just around the corner from the grave which was already attracting visitors, becoming known as the Lawrence of Arabia shrine. "Over my dead body," he told his churchwardens.

The simple church at Turners Puddle, where the River Piddle runs through the heath below the slope of Black Hill – south of Bere Regis but a world away from it in quietude and landscape quality – would have been much more appropriate. It was in the midst of the heathland that Lawrence loved and was, and indeed still is, the most beautiful backwater in these parts. Furthermore it was the church of the parish where Lawrence had lived; its 1,998 acres included Lawrence's Clouds Hill.

The farmer at Turners Puddle, George King Forster, said, firmly, "No". Public notoriety was again the excuse and Turners Puddle, fortunately, would remain a cul-de-sac to nowhere [Ordnance Survey map reference SY 830 934]

The Bishop of Salisbury came up with a compromise suggestion that the effigy should go into St Martin's church on the Saxon north wall at Wareham [map reference SY 923 877] which coincidentally was being restored in 1936. In Lawrence's time it still had an earth floor. Lawrence's younger brother, Arnold, agreed that St Martin's should have the effigy and was relieved that somewhere locally would accept it. The church was being repaired out of sense of historic duty rather than religious need and there were at that time no active worshippers to be offended.

Not that it is a frightening piece of work. Kennington wanted to convey a look of peace and the impression of the sands of Arabia rippling in wind-blown dunes. To a later generation it is that, the lines of the desert that

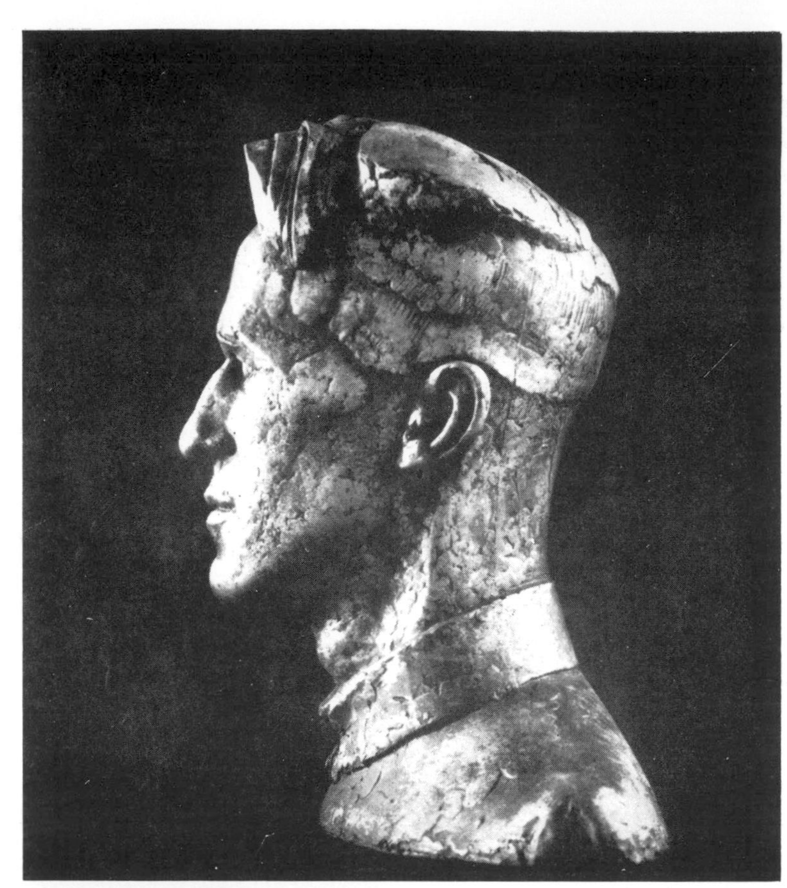

Eric Kennington created the physical images of Lawrence for posterity: he is seen working away on the life-size effigy that Moreton's rector refused to have in his church.

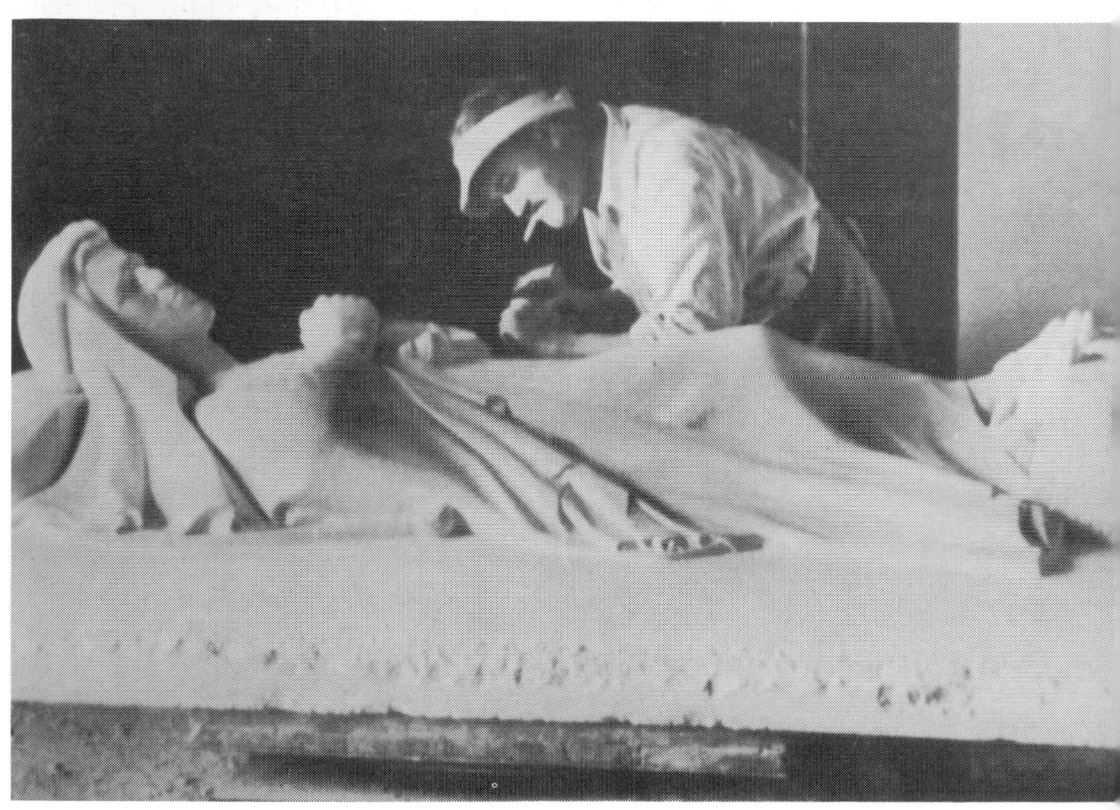

David Lean captured in the 1960s and put to Maurice Jarre's music in his masterpiece *Lawrence of Arabia*. The stone itself is sandy-looking which as Kennington observed, does have the advantage of being easy to carve.

He shows Lawrence smooth and supine at rest in the Prince of Mecca guise – with the chief's kuffieh, the curved gold-hafted dagger that he sold to Lionel Curtis; his loose flowing dress; the sandals he wore everywhere from the desert to Cairo. It is the most famous customised British army dress of all time. Captain Lawrence is enjoying a good war.

His pillow is a camel saddle. A camel whip is at his side. His sandals are propped against a Hittite carving. That, obviously, represents his interest in antiquities which came in so useful as a cover for espionage. His other passion, for learning, is indicated by the books at his head. These three titles accompanied him through the Desert Revolt – *The Oxford Book of English Verse,* Malory's *Mort d'Arthur*, and a Greek anthology.

Catchpole: the eye-witness shoots himself

An aside to the Lawrence story is the mystery death of the only independent witness to his crash, Corporal Ernest Catchpole.

L. M. Foot wrote to us from 1 Birchwood Road, Upton, after publication of the Dorset County Magazine article on Lawrence's death: "It is the first description I have read which, to some extent, resembles my hazy recollections regarding the incident and the reference to the 'black car'.

"I was also serving with the Ordnance Corps at Bovington at that time and was (fairly well) acquainted with Catchpole. It is about him and his own unfortunate end which adds a further chapter to the Lawrence mystery.

"To be brief, as you may already know the facts, Catchpole ended his own life in Egypt, June–September 1940 (from memory) the reason for which still confounds me, and further adds to the Lawrence saga.

"I took over the Senior NCO's bunk or quarter in which Catchpole met his end and many a time I lay looking at the bullet hole in the ceiling wondering what made him do such a thing and thinking it was the last link with the Lawrence incident."

The mystery flowers

"In Memory of T.E.S. 2020 AD" read the card which always accompanied a bunch of white roses that appeared each year on the grave of Dorset's "mystery man of the twentieth century" as the press continually dubbed desert hero Lawrence of Arabia. The initials on the bouquet in Moreton cemetery were for T. E. Shaw, an alias adopted by deed poll, which was the name he used whilst in Bovington with the Tank Corps and living in his

Lawrence in effigy like a mediaeval knight, tucked away in a tiny Dorset Saxon church – St Martin's at Wareham. Local prejudice had ensured it would not rest near his bones. The photograph is by Colin Graham.

cottage retreat at Clouds Hill.

Each year there would be one less rose. Forty-five was the original total when this particular spate of floral tributes began on 16 August 1975, which would have been Thomas Edward Lawrence's 87th birthday. Twenty-seven were in the bunch for 1993 – continuing the sequence for count-down to a final single rose in 2020.

They were delivered by florist Mrs Rosemarie Wise. The order arrived annually at her shop in Weymouth from the United States, via Interflora, with instructions that she was also to take a single white rose, in bud, to the cottage at Clouds Hill where Lawrence lived from 1923 until he was fatally injured nearby in an inexplicable motor-cycle accident on 13 May 1935.

Mrs Wise had no knowledge as to the identity of the mystery admirer. In 1990, the bouquet was linked to Californian doctor Susan Lawrence "who bears a striking resemblance to her hero" and visited the grave on Lawrence's birthday. However, she denied sending the flowers and said that their arrival at the same time was purely coincidental.

The mystery deepened in 1994 when Mrs Wise failed to receive her usual instructions and no birthday flowers appeared.

Not that Lawrence's grave had gone without tributes for long. Earlier in the year, on 23 April (which is St George's Day), Sunflowers of Salisbury Street, Blandford, delivered a bouquet: "To T.E.L. from your Wessex friends and a very special one – A.R."

The current flower mystery – of the significance of 2020 and the unknown cause of its earlier demise – joins an earlier floral puzzle. That one I can answer.

T. E. Lawrence's previous devoted admirer in California was Theodora Duncan who collected his works and letters and worshipped his memory. In 1968 she admitted to me that she had been the mystery lady who had added another wrapping to the Lawrence enigma by having flowers placed on his grave during the early 1960s.

"There is one more bit of information that may interest you," Miss Duncan wrote. "Another friend was 'doing Dorset' about four years ago, and she was on a bus that passed the Moreton graveyard where T.E.L. is buried. The bus driver was telling the passengers about various things they were seeing, and he commented that 'a mysterious lady from America' had put flowers on Lawrence's grave every year.

"My friend knew that I was that 'mysterious lady'. My friend Commander Frampton took care of the matter for me, for about five years.

"Then I stopped, since I felt T.E. would rather the money went to feed some hungry person."

In my book *Lawrence of Arabia in Dorset,* from which this title has evolved, I record a personal sighting of a flower on the grave and outlined the possible hidden meaning behind it being a rose: "On the June day in 1968 when I visited the grave someone had left a single red rose in front of the stone. It was the rose that all true Englishmen are supposed to obtain, with such difficulty, for the unseasonal St George's Day. Lawrence, at that moment, lay literally *sub rosa*. As an idiom for secrecy 'under the rose' has been in use since the seventeenth century. The significance of the rose as an emblem is something any member of the Secret Service would instantly recognise. I would never trust a man with a discreet rose on his tie."

Clouds Hill: the Bedouin ghost

Another aside to the story is that Clouds Hill has its ghost. He is not T. E. Lawrence but Auda abu Tayi [more properly Awdah abu-Tayyi], the savage chieftain of the Howeitat tribe who were the mainstay of Lawrence's Bedouin army. "The greatest fighting man in northern Arabia," Lawrence called him. His contribution was crucial in the capture of Akaba [more properly Aqaba]. The story was passed to me by Theodora Duncan, writing on 21 July 1968 from 1227 North Crescent Heights Boulevard in Los Angeles. She had just seen the first two issues of my Dorset County Magazine: "I would be delighted with the magazine even if you had nothing about Lawrence in it, but of course, as you say – Dorset is Lawrence Country, so ...

"I can offer this ghost story. Several years ago a friend was visiting Clouds Hill and since it was near closing time for visitors, she left the building. In the garden she noticed an old gentleman start up the stairs, so that he might enjoy Clouds Hill in some solitude, now that the crowd was leaving. In a moment, however, he came running down the stairs, very frightened, looking very greenish.

"My friend asked him what was wrong. He replied, gasping: 'I've just seen Auda abu Tayi in the upper room!' And with that he ran out into the garden.

"The letter setting forth this tale is in my collection."

Was Manning really Lawrence's 'commanding officer'?

Many whose lives were briefly touched by T. E. Lawrence would dine out on the experience for the rest of their days. One such was Air Commodore (Frederick) John Manning [1912–88], to whom departing Senior Aircraftman Shaw gave an Augustus John print of himself, inscribed: "To my last commanding officer, only wishing he were still."

They were working on air-sea rescue boats and John Manning's obituary in The Times of 12 December 1988 would have the headline "T. E. Lawrence's last CO in the RAF".

It goes on to say that "Manning had come to the RAF in 1934 via the P&O Steamship Company, and the Royal Naval reserve". That would give him only a matter of months to become a commanding officer.

The date is confirmed by *Who's Who*, which states that he entered the RAF as a Pilot Officer in 1934 and became Flight-Lieutenant in 1938, three years after Lawrence's death. *The Air Force List* shows that number 34118 FL F. J. Manning received his seniority on 22 June 1938.

Rapid promotion then ensued and when he achieved acting Air Commodore in 1944, as Director of Organisation (Establishments) at the Air Ministry, he was said to be youngest to hold that rank. The obituary is in error in saying he was then Director of Manning; that pun on his name particularly amused him – he became Manning of Manning, running the ministry's personnel department – but he held that post at the ministry towards the end of his career, in 1960–63.

Anyone checking R.A.F. lists should be warned that there is a second, older, Air Commodore Manning – Edye Rolleston Manning [1889–1957]. As for Lawrence's sickly friend Frederic Manning, of *Her Privates We*, he died shortly before Lawrence, in February 1935.

The Knowles graves at Moreton

There are gravestones in Moreton cemetery to Patrick Thomas Knowles, "Pat of Clouds Hill", who died on 30 May 1981, aged 74. Closer to T. E. Lawrence, in terms of grave spacings, is a memorial to Sergeant Pilot Bill Knowles of the Royal Air Force who was killed on 10 May 1940. He was the son of Henrietta and Arthur Knowles.

It would be interesting to know more about the young man, particularly as the day he died was one of the milestones of the Second World War. On it, Hitler moved into the Low Counties, and as a result, in London that afternoon, Neville Chamberlain's government fell and Winston Churchill became Prime Minister.

The boy who thought he had been hit by Lawrence

Ralph Neville Jones, the coroner for the Eastern Division of Dorset, held the inquest into the death of "Thomas Edward Shaw" on 21 May 1935 at the Military Hospital, Bovington Camp. He took down "Information from Witnesses" in his own hand but in each case ensured that the witness signed the notes, thereby turning them into the depositions reproduced in this book.

In 1989 a copy of one of the signatures, that of Albert Hargraves – the pedal-cyclist who was in collision with Lawrence's motor-cycle – came as a shock for Mrs E. H. Harfield of Tolworth, Surrey.

It opened a new mystery in the continuing saga of the death-crash investigations, because her late husband constantly claimed that he was the boy cyclist whom Lawrence had hit. Herbert Harfield, who was an E.N.S.A. [Entertainments National Service Association] forces performer and always used his stage name, Freddie Harfield, used to tell people of his time in Bovington Military Hospital in 1935 and of the lasting damage to his sight that was caused by the accident.

Publication of my book on *Lawrence of Arabia in Dorset* prompted Mrs Harfield to write to me about the effect the crash had on her husband's life. She had not realised there was any difference in the surnames and was amazed to see proof that it was indeed another boy who had appeared at the inquest: "On seeing the way the 'H' in Hargraves was written compared with one in my husband's signature I realised they were totally different. I just don't understand why he lied, which is totally alien to my knowledge of him, as black was black and white was white."

She insists that her Freddie suffered a serious injury in Dorset in 1935, with the lasting evidence being that his optical nerve was severed: "His parents have both passed on and I can only surmise that he thought and put himself in that boy's place and in the end really came to believe in the tale."

The belief that Lawrence never died

There is an ultimate postscript that transcends the memories and takes Lawrence of Arabia into everlasting legend. For great heroes never die. The return of Jesus is a Christian imperative. King Arthur, it was widely believed, would one day come back to save Britain.

And so, thought some, T. E. Lawrence could not really be dead. It was an opinion that even in the second half of the twentieth century could find its way into at least one newspaper. Harold J. Greenberg's "Talk of the Town" column on page 11 of the Majorca Daily Bulletin for Tuesday 30 September 1969 relays the claim of Princess de Rohan, a member of the family descended from kings of Brittany, that Lawrence was still alive and that she had met him. The motor-cycle accident was an elaborate fake set-up by the British government so that T. E. Lawrence could be drafted into the secret intelligence services.

If, however, there is a permanent place beyond the words that is forever Lawrence it is among those great banks of rhododendrons that smother the sandy knoll a mile north of Bovington Camp, with their yearly spectacle of outrageous purple to enliven the natural tawny shades of the Dorset heath. There, like E. M. Forster, I have heard the nightjar and watched for green woodpeckers in the pines. The spirit of Lawrence did not leave to go to the grave in an alien meadow of a very different Moreton landscape that in a couple of miles loses it empathy with the sands of Arabia. Clouds Hill, as it says on the map, is "Lawrence of Arabia's Cottage". As Forster put it, "The real framework, the place which he will never cease to haunt, is Clouds Hill."

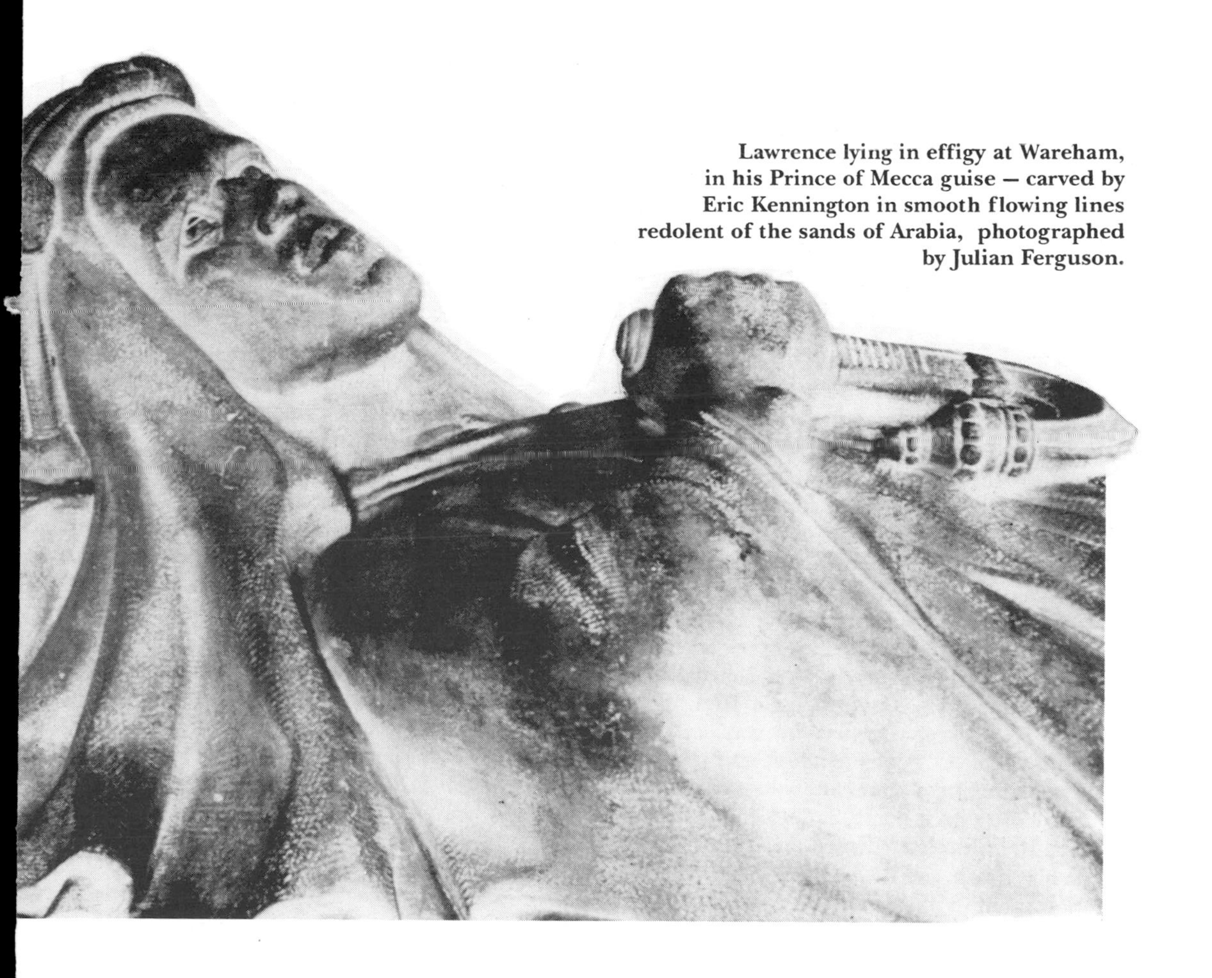

Lawrence lying in effigy at Wareham, in his Prince of Mecca guise – carved by Eric Kennington in smooth flowing lines redolent of the sands of Arabia, photographed by Julian Ferguson.

The classic Lawrence: by Augustus John.

Index

Clouds Hill: drawn by Tony Blandford, in 1968